Juliet Menéndez

LATINITAS

Celebrating 40 Big Dreamers

GODWINBOOKS

Henry Holt and Company • New York

Henry Holt and Company, *Publishers since 1866*
Henry Holt® is a registered trademark of Macmillan Publishing Group, LLC
120 Broadway, New York, NY 10271 • mackids.com

Our books may be purchased in bulk for promotional, educational, or business use.
Please contact your local bookseller or the Macmillan Corporate and Premium Sales Department at
(800) 221-7945 ext. 5442 or by email at MacmillanSpecialMarkets@macmillan.com.

Library of Congress Cataloging-in-Publication Data is available.

First edition, 2021
Book design by Liz Dresner
Printed in China by Toppan Leefung Printing Ltd., Dongguan City, Guangdong Province
The illustrations in this book were hand-painted with Old Holland watercolors on Aquarelle Arches
paper and then edited digitally with Photoshop to add the text. The font used in the illustrations is
"Mindset," designed by Erica Jung and Ricardo Marcin from Pintassilgo Prints in Brazil.

ISBN 9781250234629 (hardcover)
1 3 5 7 9 10 8 6 4 2

To my students and all Latinitas,
especially mi sobrinita, Lucía.

Table of Contents

Mercedes Sosa 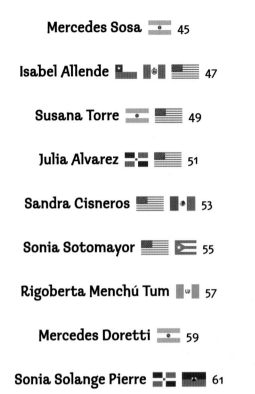 45

Isabel Allende 47

Susana Torre 49

Julia Alvarez 51

Sandra Cisneros 53

Sonia Sotomayor 55

Rigoberta Menchú Tum 57

Mercedes Doretti 59

Sonia Solange Pierre 61

Justa Canaviri 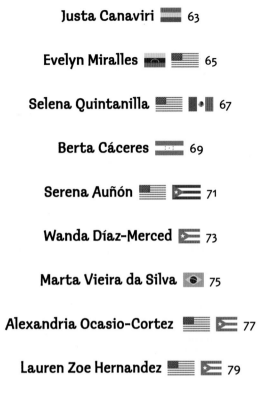 63

Evelyn Miralles 65

Selena Quintanilla 67

Berta Cáceres 69

Serena Auñón 71

Wanda Díaz-Merced 73

Marta Vieira da Silva 75

Alexandria Ocasio-Cortez 77

Lauren Zoe Hernandez 79

More Latinitas

Leona Vicario 80

Petronila Angélica Gómez 80

Hermelinda Urvina 80

Eva Perón 80

Mirabal sisters 81

Sylvia Mendez 81

Sara Gómez 81

Verónica Michelle Bachelet 81

Gloria Estefan 81

Ellen Ochoa 81

Introduction

The Latinas you will read about on these pages are women I love, respect, and admire. I wish I had discovered them when I was a child! I am lucky to have spent my days and nights getting to know them since 2014, and I am so happy to finally get the chance to share each of their incredible stories with you.

When I first had the idea for this book, I was working as an art teacher in Upper Manhattan. Like me, most of my students at the time were bicultural and had families from places like the Dominican Republic, Puerto Rico, and Mexico. But as I walked through the halls, the posters on the walls were of historical figures like Einstein, Benjamin Franklin, and Dalí. I asked myself: What if some fresh, new faces, that looked more like my students, were up on these walls?

That set me off on a fascinating search into Latinx history, where I noticed that something very important was missing: women! Seeing their contributions pushed into the footnotes of articles and history books brought out the feminist in me, and I decided to dedicate my research to them. While digging into archives, I found so many powerful stories and realized how vital Latinas have been in shaping our history. And thanks to professors, historians, family members, and the many women who have protected the bits and pieces of their legacies, I was able to put together this book!

So, how did I choose which women to include? I thought of my students and of you, the reader. I wanted to make sure that, in these pages, each of you had a chance to find someone who looked like you, played the kinds of games you play, and dreamed the kinds of dreams you dream. That is why each of the illustrations show these Latinas when they were children. Before they were running and building our cities, presiding over our courts, flying into space, healing our sick, and singing in front of millions, they were children, taking their first unknowing steps toward the women they would later become.

The Latinas on these pages are beautiful examples of the kinds of people I admire for their attitudes toward life, and the ways in which so many of them have supported their communities and contributed to future generations. I hope you are inspired by the activists and politicians fighting for us to live in a world where everyone is treated with respect and dignity, by the mathematicians and scientists whose groundbreaking work you can build upon, and by the artists, dancers, and musicians who have helped all of us find ways to understand one another.

You will find stories that go as far back as the 1650s and meet Latinas from all over Latin America and the United States who have chosen many different paths—from artists and singers like Frida Kahlo and Selena Quintanilla to congresswomen, archaeologists, and engineers like Alexandria Ocasio Cortez, Zelia Nuttall, and Evelyn Miralles. Each story is only a small glimpse into the lives of these wonderful women, and this book is only a small glimpse into the Latinas that make up our history. There is so much more for you to know and there are so many more Latinas for you to discover!

For now, I hope you enjoy seeing how your ancestors and the women around you have helped to pave the way for you to follow your own dreams. Keep their words, discoveries, and ideas alive by sharing their stories and celebrating their names. ¡Que vivan las Latinitas!

LATINITAS

Celebrating 40 Big Dreamers

SOR JUANA INÉS DE LA CRUZ

WRITER PHILOSOPHER

Sor Juana Inés de la Cruz

November 12, 1651—April 17, 1695

Ever since she was a little girl sneaking into the cornfields to read forbidden books from her abuelo's library in Mexico, Juana Inés dreamed of going to college. When she was seven and found out that college was only for boys, she begged her mother to cut off her braids and disguise her in boys' clothes so she could go. But her mother didn't dare. "Niñas aren't allowed to go to school," she declared.

"I'll teach myself, then," she said, and Juana Inés learned everything from writing poetry and prose to science and the Aztec language of Nahuatl. By the age of eight, she won a writing contest and not only got to see her first play performed, but won a book, too!

By the time she was sixteen, news of her brilliant mind had traveled to the ears of the viceroy, who refused to believe that a woman could be so smart. "I'll show her!" he thought, and invited every respected academic in Mexico to test what she knew. But Juana Inés got every single question right! She was offered a place on the viceroy's royal court and received many marriage proposals, too. But none of that was what Juana Inés really wanted to do. "Where can I go to write?" she wondered, and suddenly, she thought of just the place: a convent!

In the peace and quiet of her nun's cell, Juana Inés wrote poetry and plays by candlelight. Her ink-stained fingers filled page after page with witty critiques of the men in power and the church teachings that tried to keep women out. She sent her manuscripts off to Spain to be published, and with the help of her fellow nuns, turned the convent into a theater. She put on hilarious comedies for the royal court and thinkers of the time, artfully weaving in her feminist messages. Before long, her ideas were sparking lively debates that traveled far beyond the convent's walls. And, almost four centuries later, those very ideas are read and talked about by new generations, still inspiring change.

JUANA AZURDUY

MILITARY LEADER

Juana Azurduy de Padilla

Juana was seven when her mother died and she had to leave her school in the city to be with her papi on his hacienda. Under the hot sun of Southern Bolivia, she worked on the fields side by side with the Aymara and Quechua workers. She made friends with them and learned to speak their languages. When her papi had time, he taught her to ride horses and to shoot. He didn't think to teach her to cook or sew like most girls learned at the time.

When Juana was a teenager, her papi died and she was sent off to a convent to become a nun. But that wasn't the life Juana wanted and she escaped one night to head home. When she got back, everything had changed. All her friends from the fields were working at the Spanish silver mines. They told Juana horrible stories about how the Spanish would beat them and force them to work long hours. Juana knew she had to do something to help.

Her childhood neighbor and friend had become a rebel in the revolutionary Army of the North, and she decided to join, too. The two of them married and went off to battle together to fight against the Spanish rulers. Because of her outspoken devotion to the cause, Juana quickly became the voice of the revolution. With her Aymara and Quechua friends, she recruited over ten thousand troops! And before long, she was the one leading them into battle. She was so good at strategizing that her troop, the Loyal Battalions, won against the Spanish with only a few stolen guns, slingshots, and wooden spears! A famous general was so impressed, he gave her his very own sword to honor her.

Juana led battles during the entire revolution, defeating Spanish armies time and time again. She was so committed to her troops that, even when she had to give birth, she returned to the battlefield right afterward to lead them! All her tireless efforts paid off. Bolivia won the war for independence, and to this day, she is honored with parades and tributes every year on her birthday to celebrate her courageous fight for freedom.

POLICARPA
SALAVARRIETA

SPY

Policarpa Salavarrieta

January 26, 1795—November 14, 1817

Policarpa was good at paying attention. After losing both of her parents, she stayed close by her godmother's side and did her best to watch carefully and learn everything she could to help out. One day, while learning to stitch, she overheard her brothers talking: "We won't have our dignity until Colombia is free. We must rebel against Spain!"

"I want to be a rebel, too!" Policarpa announced. But it was the early 1800s, and her brothers told her that only boys were allowed in the army. One night, while she was lying in bed, she suddenly had an idea: if she couldn't join the army, she could be a spy!

Knocking on doors where she knew the Spanish Loyalists lived, Policarpa asked for work as a seamstress. And while sewing in the corner behind trousers and shirts, she went unnoticed as she wrote down everything she heard. Before the Loyalists could make any attacks, Policarpa snuck out messages to the rebels so they would be ready to fight back. She set up a system for getting them supplies and new recruits, too. She helped in any way she could.

Then, one night, two soldiers were caught carrying messages she had sent. The Spanish Loyalists found her and sentenced her to death—unless she went to a priest and confessed. But she refused. Instead she made a speech that inspires Colombians to this day: "I may be a woman," she said, "but I am brave enough to die a million deaths for the dignity of my country. Do not forget me."

ROSA PEÑA DE GONZÁLEZ

FOUNDER OF SCHOOLS

Rosa Peña de González

1843—1899

Rosa's mami died when Rosa was very young. The only family she had left was her papi, and she loved him very much. "I want to be just like you when I grow up!" she would tell him. When her papi was sent to prison for speaking out against the unjust authorities in Paraguay, Rosa secretly sneaked him law books so that when he got out he could continue to defend his people.

Then, the War of the Triple Alliance started in Paraguay and Rosa got sent away to Argentina. Just like her papi, Rosa read everything she could, studying hard at her new school. But, one day, when she heard news from home that all the beautiful cities and towns were burning to the ground, she realized she had to go back.

Walking past the markers of the many men who had died, Rosa was scared to be home. But she knew that it was up to the women who were left to rebuild their country. And she already had ideas about where to begin. "The first thing we need is a school!" she said. And with the little she had saved, she built the very first school for girls. She called on two sisters, Adela and Celsa Speratti, for help. The three women worked together to build up their new democracy, creating a fresh, new curriculum that encouraged all children to set their minds free.

Rosa went all around the country, from pueblo to pueblo, to get the support of each community. And, before long, twenty-four schools had been built! It took many years for Paraguay to recover from the war, but as it did, thanks to Rosa's tireless efforts, all the students were prepared to become its new leaders. To this day, Rosa is celebrated as the mother of education in Paraguay.

TERESA CARREÑO

COMPOSER CONDUCTOR

· Teresa Carreño ·

December 22, 1853—June 12, 1917

From the time Teresa was a baby, humming Italian operas before she could even talk, she would create little variations on the melody that were all her own. When she started composing pieces for the piano at the age of four, people started calling her "the second Mozart." But Teresa put her foot down. "¡No! Soy Teresita the First!" she said.

When she was eight and her family moved from Caracas, Venezuela, to New York City, Teresa gave a private concert in the salon of their Second Avenue apartment. She played beautifully, but it was when she announced "Now I will invent an opera!" and did so, right on the spot, that she caught everyone's attention. The guest of honor, the famous pianist Louis Gottschalk, exclaimed: "Teresa is a genius!" And he took it upon himself to set up her first public concert.

News of Teresa's incredible talent made it all the way to the ears of Abraham Lincoln, who invited her to play at the White House! And much to her parents' surprise, Teresa's variations on his favorite song, "Listen to the Mocking Bird," ended up bringing tears to the president's eyes.

Teresa's unique style and beautiful compositions delighted crowds from South Africa to Australia to Berlin. Orchestras from every major city in Europe invited her to play with them. When she got older, she brought out the best in many of the world's most promising pianists with her teaching. By the end of her life, Teresa had composed seventy-five pieces for piano, voice, and orchestra. She was one of the greatest, most famous, and most inspiring musicians of her time.

ZELIA
NUTTALL

ARCHAEOLOGIST

Zelia Nuttall

September 6, 1857—April 12, 1933

Zelia fell in love with ancient Mexico on her seventh birthday when her mother gave her a very special present: the hand-painted edition of *Antiquities of Mexico*. It was unlike any of the other books they had in their home library in San Francisco. The small window into her mother's country, filled with exciting illustrations of gods and goddesses in colorful headdresses, left Zelia's imagination racing with questions about these fantastic figures and how the people who believed in them might have lived. "Come out and play!" her brothers and sisters would say, but Zelia couldn't put her new treasure down.

For years, Zelia went to every dusty library she could find. By the time she was twenty, she had discovered so much about ancient Mexico that her findings were actually published! Museum curators were so impressed with her work that she was invited to travel the world collecting artifacts for their exhibitions.

On one trip, while digging up ruins on the Isla de Sacrificios in Mexico, a well-known archaeologist who was secretly a smuggler tried to steal her work. But Zelia wasn't about to let him get away with it! She wrote a forty-two-page article in the most popular archaeology journal, exposing his fraud and revealing her own extraordinary findings. To this day, Zelia's article is still considered one of the most valuable works on ancient Mexican civilizations ever written!

Zelia brought to light amazing political systems, philosophies, and scientific discoveries that existed in Latin America long before colonists ever arrived. And by working with Indigenous communities, she inspired a whole new generation of archaeologists to protect their own heritage and unravel mysteries thousands of years old.

ANTONIA NAVARRO

TOPOGRAPHICAL ENGINEER

Antonia Navarro

1870—1891

From the time Antonia was a young girl growing up in El Salvador, she was already questioning the things people said. When her brothers' teachers told her "Girls aren't smart enough to do math," Antonia went ahead and tried it anyway. Watching her single mother raise her and her brothers, Antonia learned to believe in herself.

She taught herself algebra, technical drawing, and trigonometry, too. She hiked through the clouds, studying the craters of volcanoes and the levels of the sea. Then, in 1887, even though only men were allowed to attend universities, Antonia fought her way into the engineering school at the Universidad de El Salvador. It was there that she became fascinated with the moon.

At night from her bed, she would chart each of the moon's phases. What she wanted to see most was the harvest moon she had been told about in class. But she never saw it. "Could it be," she wondered as she calculated each angle carefully, "that this moon can't actually be seen by everybody?" With proof after proof, it became clear: there were missing facts that the European astronomers had failed to explore. One day, she announced to her professors, "There is no harvest moon in El Salvador or in many other countries around the world!"

"Who does this señorita think she is?" her professors said. But seeing her thesis with detailed calculations and drawings, they had to agree: Antonia had made history. Her proofs were published in the newspaper, and she became the first woman in all of Central America to graduate from university! News of her discovery traveled all around the world, reminding mathematicians and scientists alike how important it is to challenge assumptions when new facts come to light.

MATILDE HIDALGO

COUNCILWOMAN
DOCTOR
SUFFRAGETTE

✦ Matilde Hidalgo ✦

September 29, 1889—February 20, 1974

When the nuns tried to shame Matilde in the town square, they said, "What this girl wants is wrong!" But Matilde stood strong. When mothers rushed their children indoors as she went by, Matilde held her head high. And when the boys at her school tried to put her down, Matilde stood her ground.

Everything started the day Matilde announced, "I want to be a doctor when I grow up!" Working with the nuns at a nearby hospital, she loved knowing how to help people and dreamed of opening a clinic where rich and poor patients were treated side by side. But as a girl in 1907, Matilde had to fight just to be allowed to go to university.

As the only girl studying medicine, Matilde spent her first days at university eating lunch all alone. She took that time to study and write poetry, crafting clever replies to all the boys who teased her in class. Before long, she was earning excellent grades and putting those boys in their place. She made many friends and finally earned the respect she deserved. She became the first woman to graduate from medical school in Ecuador!

One day, Matilde got to open her clinic, saving the lives of countless families that couldn't afford to pay. Whenever Matilde encountered injustice or inequality, she fought against it. She not only became the first woman to vote in all of Latin America but also won the trust of the very neighbors who had shunned her as a girl. Eventually, she became the first elected councilwoman in Ecuador! From then on, thanks to Matilde's bravery, women from all over Latin America saw the many possibilities their futures could hold.

GABRIELA MISTRAL
TEACHER WRITER

Gabriela Mistral

April 7, 1889—January 10, 1957

Gabriela's father left her family when Gabriela was very young. But before he left, he planted a garden. It was nestled between Chile's Andes Mountains and an olive grove, and Gabriela grew up there alongside the birds and flowers. While her mother worked long hours and her sister taught school, Gabriela spent her days running around the roots of the fig trees and playing under the almond flowers. Gabriela loved this little corner of the world so much that she tried to put her love into words. Writing verses to the rhythm of the wind and the songs of the birds, she composed her first poems.

Gabriela grew up to do many wonderful things. She became a famous teacher, traveling to schools throughout Latin America and the United States. She worked as a journalist who defended equality and women's rights. Later, she even became a consul representing Chile around the world. Everywhere she went, from Mexico to Italy, Greece, France, and the United States, she kept on writing. And no matter where she was, she loved to look out of her window at the sky and imagine herself back home. Even through some of her most difficult times, she never stopped writing about her love for that special valley of her childhood. Book by book, she left little pieces of it in the hearts of readers from all over the world.

Gabriela's writing won her the Nobel Prize in Literature in 1945. She was the very first Latin American and only the fifth woman in the whole world to win it! "This award belongs to my homeland," she said, and accepted it on Chile's behalf. And when she died, she left all the money she had earned from her books and prizes to the children of her beloved valley.

JUANA
DE IBARBOUROU

WRITER

Juana de Ibarbourou

March 8, 1892—July 15, 1979

One morning, when Juana came down for breakfast, her mami said, "Hija, go put that sheet back on your bed!"

"But, Mami, if I take off my purple cloak, how will the prince know it's me?"

Her mami laughed and laughed. "I don't see what's so funny," Juana said. But as she ate up her tostadas and drank her cafe con leche, she began to wonder: "Does Mami really not understand?"

It wasn't until Juana's mami looked at the swirled stain of paint on her wall and said she couldn't see the monkeys swinging from the jungle trees, nor did she know anything about the little gnomes who came in the night to make their morning panecito rise, that Juana understood: son secretos.

Juana kept her magic bottled up like the caterpillars and ladybugs she would catch in jars outside. But when she was fourteen, she found the perfect way to set it free. In her first sonnet, about a little lamb that came to her in dreams, she started to put together words and images that she had been collecting like treasures. Day after day, she wrote. And by the time she was seventeen, she had written enough poems to fill a book!

While World War I was weighing heavily on everyone's hearts, Juana's book came out and gave everyone in Uruguay the perfect escape. "Let's go to the campo," she wrote in one poem. "Take my hand." And her readers followed her, walking through memories of simpler times when grass and fig trees perfumed the air, magos carried cures, and church bells marked the hour. People from all over Latin America loved her and her work so much that they gave her the name Juana de América!

⁚ Pura Belpré ⁚

February 2, 1903—July 1, 1982

Ever since Pura was a little girl in Puerto Rico, she loved listening to all the old tales her abuela would tell over afternoon cafecito. It wasn't long before she knew them by heart and all the funny voices for the characters that went along with them. At recess, under the shade of the tamarind tree, she would try them out, making her friends hug their bellies with laughter.

Years later, when she went to New York for her sister's wedding, it just so happened that the library was looking for a bilingual librarian. It was perfect! Pura dropped her plans of becoming a teacher in Puerto Rico and jumped at the chance to share stories with the newly arrived Spanish-speaking immigrants. "It's my destino!" she thought.

On her first day, she ran to the folktale section, looking for her favorite stories to read to the children. But there wasn't a single folktale from Puerto Rico! "¡Dios mío! How can this be?" she said. So she decided to write the tales herself. Her first was about a beautiful cockroach named Martina who falls in love with a stylish mouse named Pérez. The other librarians loved it so much, they asked Pura to perform it before it was even published. With handmade puppets, Pura brought Martina and Pérez to life, giving a taste of Puerto Rico to children from all over the city.

It was such a success that Pura got the great idea to invite authors from all over Latin America to share their stories and poems at the library. Before long, the library became a meeting place for Spanish-speaking readers and authors alike. They even celebrated the traditional Three Kings Day there, complete with dancing and music! Thanks to Pura and the many librarians she inspired, immigrants today still feel like the New York Public Library and libraries all over the country are their second homes.

GUMERCINDA PÁEZ

PLAYWRIGHT
CONGRESSWOMAN

: Gumercinda Páez .

January 13, 1904—1991

Gumercinda grew up in a neighborhood where everyone worked long days and long nights and still couldn't make ends meet. Even so, the upper-class Panamanians often treated the people around her with contempt for being poor. "If only they knew what it was really like . . ." Gumercinda thought. And at only ten years old, she came up with a way: "¡Ya sé! I can write plays about our lives!" Getting her neighbors and amigos to act out the parts, Gumercinda put on play after play.

But the only people seeing Gumercinda's plays were her own neighbors. "How will I get these plays to the rest of Panama?" she wondered. When she grew up and became a teacher, Gumercinda came up with a plan: she could make her plays into radionovelas and ask her students to be the actors!

Before long, stories of fathers forced to leave their families for work, single mothers making incredible sacrifices, grandmothers working well into their old age, and children working when they should have been in school were seen all across Panama. The upper classes finally saw what life was really like for most people, and Gumercinda's community finally got a chance to feel understood. In only a few years, Gumercinda wrote thirty-four radionovelas!

Gumercinda decided to run for office and not only became the first Black woman to win, she got elected as the vice president of the constitutional assembly, too! Coming into politics right after the political coup of 1941, she helped draft Panama's new constitution, and the very issues at the center of her radionovelas became the pillars of her work. She fought for and won equal pay for women, public daycare for children, paid maternity leave, and the recognition of Afro-Latinx rights. And she didn't stop there! Gumercinda traveled all over Latin America defending human rights. Now there is an award given every year in her name to women who carry on her incredible legacy.

FRIDA
KAHLO

ARTIST

: Frida Kahlo :.

July 6, 1907—July 13, 1954

When Frida was six years old, she got polio and had to stay in bed for months with nothing to do. During those long hours, she would imagine what it would be like to jump through her window and explore the city outside. Then, one day, she drew a little door on the glass and, like magic, she created an entire world of her own! She loved her imaginary world full of wild animals and beautiful flowers so much that, even when she got better, she would find quiet moments to go back through that little door.

When Frida was eighteen, she got into a terrible bus accident coming home from school. Again, she was forced to stay in bed. Only this time, instead of keeping her world locked up in her imagination, Frida decided to paint it so others could peek inside. With a special easel made just for her bed, she painted colorful self-portraits filled with animals, flowers, magic, and ghosts. When she could walk again, she took all her paintings to the famous mural painter Diego Rivera. When she asked him if they were any good, he said, "They are even better than mine!"

Little did she know that years later she and Diego would get married! Together, they traveled the world, and everywhere they went, people were fascinated with Frida and the fantastic world of her paintings. Frida's work was shown in San Francisco, Boston, and New York and became part of the Louvre Museum's collection in Paris!

Frida loved traveling, but what she wanted most was to come home and show her work in Mexico. Many years passed before her dream finally came true, and by that time, Frida was very sick and was ordered by her doctor to stay in bed. But she couldn't miss her show, so she put on her best dress and decided to go, bed and all! Swaying on the shoulders of her friends and family, she proudly looked up at her two hundred paintings hanging on the walls.

JULIA DE BURGOS

POET

Julia de Burgos

February 17, 1914—July 6, 1943

Listening to her father rattle off lines from famous poets as the two of them trotted through the forests of Puerto Rico on horseback, Julia began to discover the rhythms and rhymes of words. Soon she was thinking and speaking like a poet. She would braid the grass and say, "I'm curling the campo's hair!" Julia loved words so much that writing verses with her little sister Consuelo was her favorite game to play.

Julia was the oldest of thirteen brothers and sisters and, even though her family was very poor, she got a scholarship to go to university. There, she learned that words were more than beautiful; they could also open up people's minds to ideas like independence, equality, and human rights.

Julia became a teacher and was proud to share her ideals with the children of Puerto Rico. But her poet's heart also made itself heard. One day, while looking out on a flamboyán tree in the schoolyard, she felt so inspired that she ran out of her class. "Consuelo, can you take over for me?" she asked. As the bright morning sun came and went, she sat under the tree, writing until the very last line of her poem was done. Seeing the river of her childhood flowing in the distance, she used it as a symbol to weave her own story in with the history of her country. When Julia finally got up to show her poem, "Río Grande de Loíza," to her sister, they both immediately knew: it was a masterpiece.

Filled with a new confidence, Julia started writing day and night. When she had filled a book with her poems, she started giving readings and speaking out as a feminist supporting Puerto Rican independence. Round after round of applause inspired her to go to Cuba and then on to New York. She was an inspiration everywhere she went! And when she died, she was so loved that her fans from all over the United States and Puerto Rico created murals, lining their streets and schools with beautiful tributes to her work and life.

CHAVELA VARGAS

SINGER

Chavela Vargas

April 17, 1919—August 5, 2012

Ever since Chavela was little, people said she didn't walk, talk, or sing like a girl. She tried to fit in, but in her small town in Costa Rica, people didn't accept her being even a little bit different from the other girls her age. The priest wouldn't let her come to church on Sundays, her parents wouldn't let her come out of her room when they had visitors, and at recess, when she asked to play, the other girls would say, "¡Así no!"

It was only when Chavela would curl up by the record player to listen to Mexican rancheras that she felt like someone understood her. "One day, I'll get out of here and sing like them!" she thought. She learned all the words to every song and sang wherever she went.

When she was sixteen, she took a bus all the way to Mexico. She put on a dress, makeup, and high heels like the women singers she had seen. But on the night of her first big performance, she fell in front of the whole audience! "¡Ya basta!" Chavela declared. She got rid of the heels and put on a poncho and pants, and, from then on, no matter what anyone said, she was done trying to be anyone but herself. It was hard at first, but little by little, Chavela started to get shows. And it was her deep, rough voice and unique style that made her stand out!

Chavela recorded eighty record albums and toured far and wide, performing at places like Carnegie Hall in New York, Luna Park in Buenos Aires, and the Olympia in Paris. She gave her very last concert at age ninety-two! Before she died, she said, "I leave with Mexico in my heart." And at her funeral, Mexicans lined the streets and people came from all over the world to say goodbye and show that she was in their hearts, too.

ALICIA ALONSO

BALLERINA

Alicia Alonso

December 21, 1920—October 17, 2019

"Pay attention! Sit still!" the nuns at her Catholic school would say. But Alicia liked to be up and moving out of her seat. She was always dancing. When the famous Russian dancer Nikolai Yavorsky came to open the first ballet school in Cuba, Alicia ran to sign up. And when she got her first pair of ballet shoes, she loved them so much that she slept with them under her pillow every night.

Alicia quickly became one of Yavorsky's best students and met her first love, Fernando, in his class. At fifteen, they ran away together to New York City to chase their dreams of becoming world-famous dancers.

But just as her career was taking off, Alicia started losing her sight. She had to have surgery, and while she lay in bed recovering for months, she asked Fernando to draw the dance steps for the upcoming show, *Giselle*, in the palm of her hand. Before long, she knew every step by heart. And even after finding out that the surgery didn't restore her sight, she was determined to continue dancing. When the prima ballerina in her troupe got sick, Alicia took her chance. "I can do it!" she said. Without being able to see, she danced the part beautifully—the best Giselle anyone had ever seen! "*Bravissima!*" the audience yelled.

Alicia went back to Cuba and founded the Ballet Nacional de Cuba. It quickly became one of the best ballet schools in the world and she kept teaching there up until she was ninety-eight years old! When she died, her students came from all over Cuba to honor her and thank her for everything she had given them before saying goodbye.

VICTORIA
SANTA CRUZ

POET
PHILOSOPHER
COMPOSER
DIRECTOR
CHOREOGRAPHER

Victoria Santa Cruz

October 27, 1922—August 30, 2014

At Victoria's home in Lima, Peru, dinnertime was a celebration. Her mother would sing and dance to African zamacueca music while she cooked. Victoria and her siblings would tap along to the rhythm with their spoons and plates. And after dessert, it was time for reciting poetry and guessing composers of classical tunes. Victoria was proud of her family and who she was.

Then one day, a new girl with blond hair and blue eyes came to Victoria's school from los Estados Unidos. At recess, Victoria and her friends were excited to play with her. But the new girl turned up her nose: "If that negra is going to play, I'm not." To Victoria's surprise, her own friends told Victoria she couldn't play with them anymore. Victoria began to wonder if there was something bad about being negra. So for years, she straightened her hair and put powder on her skin to make it lighter.

But as she grew up and began to discover bold and beautiful black artists, dancers, and composers, she felt the same pride she had felt as a little girl. With her older brother, she opened a theater featuring black musicians, dancers, and actors. Victoria composed the music, choreographed the dances, and even sewed all the costumes. Each night, more and more people came to the theater and the rounds of applause got louder and louder. And each night, Victoria stood taller, straighter, and stronger. She let her natural hair grow out and stopped putting on that powder. To celebrate her pride, she wrote a powerful poem: "Me gritaron negra."

Victoria traveled the world, teaching and performing Afro-Peruvian music and dances. When she got back to Peru, she became the director of the National Institute of Culture and went on to open another theater. This time, she showcased stories from all the different peoples of Peru. "Porque," she said, "in the end, we are all one familia."

CLARIBEL ALEGRÍA
WRITER

Claribel Alegría

May 12, 1924—January 25, 2018

At night, as the soft smell of coffee flowers drifted through their window in El Salvador, Claribel's papi would read poems from Nicaragua's famous poet Rubén Darío. To Claribel, Darío's words were like notes on a piano—lullabies from her papi's country and the land of her birth. And before she could even read, Claribel played at making her own words sound like those delicate notes, asking her mami to write down the poems she would say aloud.

Then, one night, peeking through the curtains by the side of her bed, she saw Indigenous families—women, men, and children—being pushed and shoved by military guards pointing guns to their heads. "This isn't right!" her papi yelled at the guards as he ran out the door. "Don't do this! Put down your guns!" But the guards didn't listen.

That night haunted Claribel's dreams. She kept wondering, "Who were those people? What were they like before their lives were taken away? What would they have wanted to say?"

Then one day, her papi gave her a very special gift. Wrapped neatly in a small box was an elegant pen. "You have the gift of words," he said. "Use them like swords." And that's exactly what Claribel did. Day after day, she wrote and wrote, using her delicate words to tell powerful, sharp-edged truths.

When she grew up, Claribel moved from country to country meeting revolutionaries, political prisoners, and the families of desaparecidos, who had been looking for their loved ones for years. She risked her life to publish stories that were meant to have been buried or silenced with threats. She wrote until she was ninety-three, saying, "Every time I name them, my dead are resurrected." And thanks to her bravery, the names and stories of the silenced have not been forgotten and can be heard all over the world.

Celia Cruz

October 21, 1925—July 16, 2003

From the time she was a little girl, music was the most important thing in Celia's life. She loved every type there was: the songs her mother sang while making fresh plátanos, the beats from her neighbor's bembé next door, and the boleros she would hear while walking along the streets of Havana, Cuba. And she loved to sing. She knew every song on the radio by heart and was happy to sing for anyone who wanted to listen.

But one night, she discovered her very favorite kind of music. Tempted by the sounds of the carnaval wafting through her window, she snuck out with her tía to join in the fun. She couldn't believe what she saw! Everyone was dressed up in sparkling costumes and dancing and singing to salsa music everywhere she went. It felt like magic. And when she got back home, she had the most wonderful dream she had ever had: she was wearing a flowing white dress and she was the queen of the carnaval!

Celia never forgot that dream, and when she grew up, she put on that beautiful white dress she had imagined and auditioned to sing for her favorite salsa band, La Sonora Matancera. They fell in love with her voice, and before long everyone in Cuba did, too. Her dream came true! Only, instead of becoming the queen of the carnaval, she became the salsa queen. "¡Azúcar!" she would shout out. Life was sweet.

Celia's voice became the sound of salsa, and she won Grammy Award after Grammy. She traveled all over the world giving concerts, moved to the United States, recorded more than seventy albums, and even got her own star on the Hollywood Walk of Fame! To this day, if there is salsa dancing at a party and it feels like "la vida es un carnaval," one of her songs is sure to be playing.

DOLORES HUERTA

ACTIVIST

Dolores Huerta

April 10, 1930—present

As a little girl, Dolores lived in California between the orchards and vineyards where her mami owned a hotel. Dolores watched her mami scrimp and save to make ends meet. But whenever farmworkers came and needed a place to sleep, her mami let them stay for free. When people needed help, she'd always find a way.

Just like her mami, when soldiers' families were left without their papis during World War II, Dolores got together with her Girl Scout troop to find a way to help. Fundraising on the streets, they helped the families buy clothes and food.

Dolores grew up to become a schoolteacher. But when her students would come to class hungry and without shoes on their feet, she knew the work she needed to do should start with their parents: the farmworkers. Dolores went to the fields and found them living in shacks with dirt floors. They didn't even have clean water to drink! But they were too afraid to complain. Dolores insisted, "If we all stand up together, we can create change!" She teamed up with another organizer, César Chavez, and founded the very first farmworkers union in the United States!

Together, Dolores and César led protests and rallies. They talked to Congress. They even got a presidential candidate on their side. But when the growers didn't listen, Dolores decided to go to New York and organize a boycott. She called on her feminist, Puerto Rican, and Black Panther allies, and together they got seventeen million people not to buy grapes. That sure got the growers' attention! The farmworkers could finally negotiate decent working conditions and wages! Everyone said it couldn't be done, but Dolores kept saying, "¡Sí se puede!"—and she was right! Even President Barack Obama used her famous slogan for his campaign, because there's nothing people can't do when they come together and take a stand. ¡Sí se puede! Yes we can!

Rita Rosita Moreno

December 11, 1931—present

At five years old, Rosita was happy playing under the warm sun of Juncos, Puerto Rico, cooking pretend feasts in her cacerolitas. But when her mami decided to start a new life in New York, everything changed. As soon as Rosita set foot on the freezing cold city streets filled with gangs at the ready with insults and pipes, she got the message loud and clear: "You don't belong here!" "I want to go back to our casita!" Rosita would cry.

Then, one day, the sun came back and the flowers bloomed. Rosita felt happy for the first time and twirled all around the room. "You could be a dancer!" her mother exclaimed, and she signed Rosita up for classes with the famous Spanish dancer Paco Cansino. Rosita loved moving her feet to the rhythms of the classic Sevillanas and dressing up in the elaborate costumes her mami stitched by hand. By nine, she was already giving her first performance in Greenwich Village, and by nineteen she was off to Hollywood!

It seemed like a dream come true. But after being told to change her hair, her makeup, and her name to Rita, too, and still not getting the roles she deserved, she wondered, "Am I just not good enough?" Then, an exciting new musical, *West Side Story*, came out and she got to play a Puerto Rican for the first time in her life. She danced and sang and acted her heart out. And she won an Oscar for her role!

Finally, the world got to see how beautiful and talented she had been all along. Rita went on to win a Grammy, an Emmy, and a Tony, and she is still acting! Now, with her name among the stars, she is right where she belongs.

Maria Auxiliadora da Silva

May 24, 1935—August 20, 1974

From the time Maria was a little girl, she found art everywhere she looked. Even the coal from the kitchen stove got her mind whirling with ideas.

"Is dinner almost ready?" her mamãe would call out.

"¡Ai ai ai!" Maria would say with a start, running from her charcoal drawing on the wall to save the food she was supposed to be watching from being burned to a crisp.

When Maria's mamãe saw the food, she just laughed. She understood. She was an artist, too. When Maria was nine, it was her mother who taught her all the different stitches for embroidery and how to work with colors. "Vem, sit with me," her mother would say, and together they would tell stories with their threads.

When Maria grew up, she made her stories into paintings, mixing in the patterns and textures her mother taught her. Just as she had when she was a little girl, she could turn anything into art, even her own hair! She invented all her own techniques, building up parts of her paintings like a sculpture and playing with perspectives and colors like no one had done before. And by including little conversation bubbles where her figures made comments about education, feminism, racism, religion, and politics, she invited the public to talk. When art critics and academics tried to put labels on her or her work, she didn't let them. "I am an artist," she would say, and leave it at that.

Maria did everything on her own terms. By refusing to fit into offensive categories that made her feel like an outsider, she inspired a new generation of Brazilians who no longer measure themselves against European standards, but instead create their own. Maria was so full of fresh ideas that, even when she got very sick, she never stopped making art. When she died of cancer at age thirty-nine, she was working on a drawing that very day. Her family found it lying under her pillow.

MERCEDES SOSA
SINGER

: Mercedes Sosa .

July 9, 1935—October 4, 2009

High up in the trees of the park by her house in Tucumán, Argentina, Mercedes would sit and think. While everyone played down below, her empty stomach would grumble and she would ask herself: "How is it that Mami and Papi work so hard and can't make enough money for us to eat? Why is it that people who look like me always seem to be the ones who are poor?"

Listening to Víctor Jara's and Violeta Parra's songs on the radio, Mercedes found she wasn't the only one asking these questions. Their songs, traveling to her from Chile, felt like secret windows into her thoughts. She would sing their words to herself, filled with hope that one day things would change.

But the government didn't want anything to change, and they had Víctor Jara killed. When Mercedes heard the news, her incredible sadness and anger gave her courage. Having been told by one of her high school teachers that she had a beautiful voice, she decided to use it. She was so nervous, she couldn't look at her audience and had to close her eyes. But she sang out strong and loud. She made sure the power of Víctor Jara's words—and of all those who had dared to speak out—came through in her voice. Bigger and bigger crowds came to listen. By the time the government tried to stop Mercedes, her voice had already helped start a revolution.

Mercedes traveled all over Latin America and the world, singing out for women and children and human rights. Even when she received death threats, she never stopped singing. Her voice became the voice of the people. And, even today, when protestors come together, they play Mercedes' recordings, letting her voice guide them as they march through the streets.

ISABEL ALLENDE
WRITER

Isabel Allende

1942–present

Isabel grew up in her abuelos' house in Chile, which was filled with wild pets and the ghosts her abuela summoned during séances. At night, her abuelo loved to recite epic poems and fabulous folktales. For Isabel, it was the most magical place.

But when Isabel was ten, her mother remarried and the two of them had to follow her stepfather as he traveled the world for work. Isabel packed every object, smell, and memory of the rooms at her abuelos' house into her heart. And during lonely, homesick nights, she would travel back there in her dreams.

Right when Isabel was going to finally return to her abuelos' house, a brutal political coup in Chile forced her to stay abroad for her safety. Far away and missing her home more than ever, she received a phone call: "Your abuelo is very sick." With her heart breaking, she wrote him a long letter filled with all the memories she had packed away from her childhood. She wrote page after page to her dear abuelo, traveling through her words to the times and places that made up his extraordinary life and weaving in her own fantastic imagination. By the time she finished, she had written over five hundred pages!

That very long letter became her first book, *The House of the Spirits*. It was as epic as her grandfather's poems and as magical as the folktales he told. This book and the twenty-four she has written since have been translated into forty-two different languages! So even though her grandfather is no longer alive, people from all over the world get the chance to know him and all the other wonderful characters Isabel brings back to life.

SUSANA
TORRE
ARCHITECT

: Susana Torre :

November 2, 1944—present

Running through the fields in Puán, Argentina, Susana and her cousin spotted a bird building its nest. "¡Probemos!" said Susana excitedly. They went to work gathering up bunches of twigs and mud. Together, they wove a whole collection of nests and then hid them in the trees of their village plaza. "Will the birds choose ours?" they wondered, and waited in the bushes hoping to find out. But the birds always seemed to know which nests were their own. "What makes something feel like home?" Susana asked herself.

When Susana got older, she continued to ask herself that question. In an art history class, she learned about the beautiful dome of Hagia Sophia in Istanbul, Turkey. There, sitting under the spectacular wreath of windows that made the dome look like it was floating on beams of light, Christians, and later Muslims, would come together to pray. "I want to create spaces that bring people together like that!" Susana thought. "I want to be an architect!"

Susana started imagining the different kinds of places she could make. For her most famous project, Fire Station number 5 in Columbus, Indiana, she got rid of locker rooms and created shared spaces instead, with a big kitchen where everyone could meet. It was the first station in the United States to welcome women into the field, and it changed the way fire stations were built across the country!

Susana also put together the very first exhibit celebrating the brilliant work of women architects. It was so successful when it opened at the Brooklyn Museum that it traveled throughout the United States and made it all the way to the Netherlands! And to this day, for each space Susana creates, from an office building to a park, she makes sure it is a place where everyone can feel that they belong.

JULIA ALVAREZ

WRITER

Julia Alvarez

March 27, 1950—present

Sitting on her grandfather's knee telling him what she wanted to be, Julia imagined endless possibilities: "A bullfighter! A cowboy! A famous actress in Hollywood movies! I want to ride in a submarine and be a pilot and fly to Nueva York to buy toys!" she would say. And her abuelo would smile, but the side-eye he gave to her tíos and tías said it all: she would be a mamá, a tía, an abuela. Those were the dreams she was supposed to dream.

It wasn't until Julia and her family escaped President Rafael Trujillo's dictatorship in the Dominican Republic and moved to New York that Julia found a different way to be all the things she wanted to be. Hiding from the bullies who made fun of her accent and threw stones at her on the playground, Julia spent recess escaping into books. Reading book after book, she not only came to master the language of her new home but also found that she could step into the shoes of anyone she wanted to know or be!

As Julia grew up, she went from reading her way into the lives of characters to writing her way in. She wrote about the famous Mirabal sisters risking everything to overthrow President Trujillo, about doctors on a mission to save the world with vaccines, and about a Mexican family struggling to keep their undocumented status a secret in the United States.

Even though her family worried about the bold political stories she wanted to tell, Julia kept writing. Now she passes on what she learned by teaching future writers to push beyond the edges of their imaginations—and always to take a look through other people's eyes.

SANDRA CISNEROS

WRITER

: Sandra Cisneros .

December 20, 1954—present

With six rambunctious brothers running around her family's small Chicago house, Sandra was constantly on the lookout for a quiet place. The first time she stepped into the public library, where you had to be quiet and where there were nooks and crannies to curl up in—perfect for escaping into the worlds of books—she knew she had finally found it.

Sandra filled her mind with stories of people who lived in places she could only imagine and who spoke with voices unlike anyone she had ever met. She dreamed of writing books like the ones on all those shelves.

When she grew up, Sandra went off to a famous writing school in Iowa. But the more she tried to sound like the voices in the books she had read, the more she found she couldn't write. "Who are these people who have attics and summer houses by the sea?" she asked herself. And suddenly, it hit her! "What if I write about people who never find their way into these books? What if I write about people like me?"

Night after night, Sandra worked on a story that would later become known as *The House on Mango Street*. She filled it with her own voice and the voices of people she knew and loved. When it was published, it felt so true to so many people that it became an instant classic.

Now, while she writes her next book, she is working to support other writers, too. Through the Macondo Writers Workshop, which she founded, Sandra is helping writers from many different backgrounds bring their own stories to life.

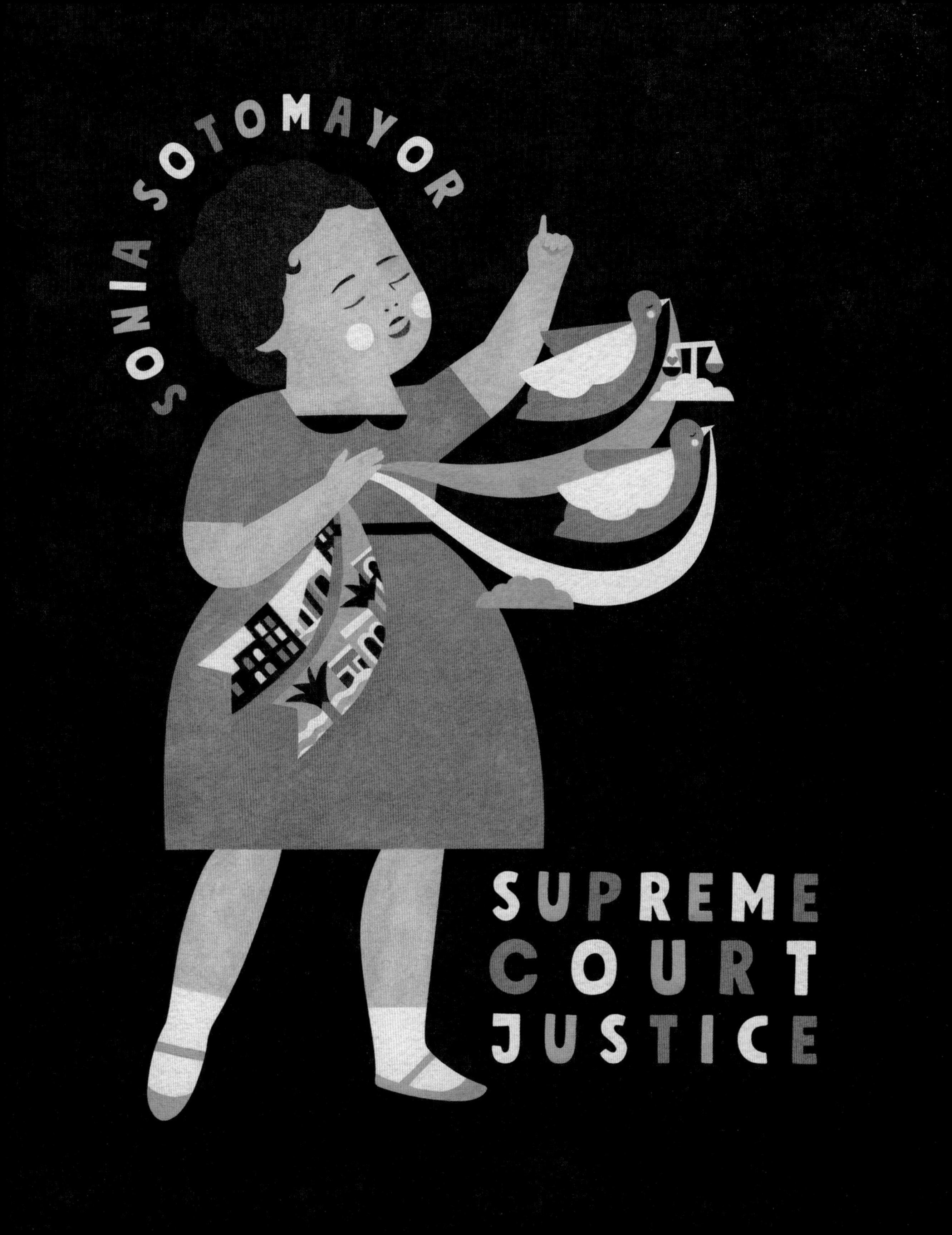
SONIA SOTOMAYOR
SUPREME
COURT
JUSTICE

Sonia Sotomayor

June 25, 1954—present

It was in her abuelita's apartment in the Bronx, with all her cousins and tíos crowded into two rooms, that Sonia learned how to get people's attention. When Abuelita stood up to recite beloved Puerto Rican poems at those family parties, even the most heated argument over dominoes would go quiet. As Abuelita's strong, deep voice made its way to everyone's hearts, Sonia's tías and tíos were moved to tears. Sonia saw how her abuelita brought words to life—not only painting pictures in people's minds, but waking up their feelings, too.

Sonia's dream was to become a lawyer like her favorite TV character, Perry Mason. She joined the debate team in high school, but at first, even with solid arguments, she lost. Then one day, she decided to channel Abuelita. Little by little, sculpting her words into pictures with her hands, Sonia built the tension. She felt the room fall silent, and soon she had the entire audience on the edge of their seats. By getting the audience to imagine themselves in someone else's place, she brought together her final argument, reaching the hearts of everybody there. As she went to step down from the stage, the whole audience broke into applause! Just like Abuelita, Sonia got everyone to not only hear her words, but feel their power. She won the debate!

Sonia became a lawyer, then a judge. She impressed everyone so much that President Barack Obama nominated her to the Supreme Court! Now, helping to decide the most important cases in the country and standing up for equal rights, Sonia never forgets that making a good argument is just as much about connecting with people as it is about choosing the right words.

RIGOBERTA MENCHÚ TUM

ACTIVIST

Rigoberta Menchú Tum

January 9, 1959—present

With her piglet and sheep, lying in watch over the growing maíz, little Rigoberta loved to dream. Under the same Guatemalan night sky where her ancestors had mapped the stars, Rigoberta dreamed of the day her pueblo of Laj Chimel would finally be able to live off of their land. Instead of taking those crowded old buses down to the fincas to pick cotton and coffee for only a few cents a day, they could stay up on the mountains of Quiché in peace.

Year after year, after long seasons breaking their backs on the finqueros' fields, the whole pueblo worked together to tend their own crops. And right around Rigoberta's fourteenth birthday, they finally grew enough to feed everyone! Rigoberta's neighbors gave thanks, playing their chirimías and drums!

But before long, the finca owners found out, and, taking advantage of the internal war that had been targeting Indigenous communities like Rigoberta's for years, they brought in the army to steal the land. Rigoberta's father, don Vicente Menchú Perez, started working with community leaders to stand up for their rights, but he got sent to jail. Rigoberta knew she had to take on la lucha. She went to work organizing meetings to come up with a plan. "¡Ke'qach'ija' na! ¡Resistimos!" she told her pueblo. And when the army came back with guns, the neighbors were ready with tricks and traps to outsmart them.

Rigoberta went all over Guatemala helping other pueblos defend their rights. Her mother, father, and brother were murdered and she was threatened, too. She was forced to leave her country, but she never gave up. In exile, she wrote her famous testimony, *I, Rigoberta Menchú*, for the whole world to see and joined the United Nations to bring her country and her community peace. She won the Nobel Peace Prize in 1992 and has been working ever since , defending Indigenous communities both in court and in the public's eye to make sure everyone is treated with respect and dignity.

MERCEDES DORETTI

FORENSIC ANTHROPOLOGIST

: Mercedes Doretti ·

1959—present

Mercedes grew up during a dangerous time in Argentina. The military was in power, and people could disappear in the night just for saying the wrong thing or even for being friends with people the military didn't like.

In the central Plaza de Mayo, abuelas would come together and demand to know what had happened to their hijos and nietos. "Are they still alive? Are they hungry or cold?" Month after month, day after day, the abuelas came. "We deserve to know!" they would say.

"I wish I could help," Mercedes thought as she passed by.

One day, in Mercedes' college anthropology class, a man from the United States walked through the door. "The abuelas asked me to come here," he said. "I am going to uncover what the military has tried to hide. Who's with me?"

Mercedes was scared. What this man was asking them to do was very different from looking at bones from ancient civilizations, like Mercedes was used to. But she knew how important it was, so she raised her hand. "I'll go," Mercedes said.

Mercedes worked with a team to dig up the bones of those who had disappeared. By analyzing them, they gave the abuelas the truth they had so long been waiting for. Finally, there was evidence to take to the courts. Mercedes was so inspired that she put together a group to continue working. She now leads projects around the world, discovering proof of crimes against humanity, and giving families who seek justice the respect they deserve. Thanks to Mercedes, truths that have been buried are getting the chance to be told.

SOLANGE PIERRE

ACTIVIST

Sonia Solange Pierre

July 4, 1963—December 4, 2011

Sonia's name wasn't Sonia. That name was just easier for her teacher to say. And her name wasn't Solain Pié, either. The Dominican officials had just registered her any old way. It didn't matter to them that her real name was Solange.

To many people living outside her batey, it didn't matter whether Solange and her neighbors had running water or schools or a hospital to go to when they got sick. People living in the batey were seen as Haitian immigrants who had come to the Dominican Republic to work in the sugarcane fields. And that was it. But Solange had other ideas.

By the time she was thirteen, she was organizing from batey to batey. "We need schools, hospitals, and decent pay! Y no vale if we don't strike together," she would say. Once, while leading a march, guards arrested her and told her mami, "Get your daughter under control or we're sending her back to Haiti!" But instead of stopping Solange, the guards' racist comments only made her more determined. "I was born Dominican! I should be treated as a full citizen!" Solange declared.

Solange organized a group of women to take the Dominican government to court in the name of all Dominico-Haitians who hadn't been given their rights as citizens. She traveled the world to get international support, and in 2005, the women won their first case with the Inter-American Court of Human Rights upholding the right for Dominico-Haitian children to have birth certificates! Finally, they would be recognized as Dominican citizens! Sadly, Solange died before the Dominican government complied, but thanks to her work, there are now schools and clinics in the bateys and an entire community committed to fighting for their rights.

JUSTA
CANAVIRI

CHEF

Justa Canaviri

August 13, 1963—present

Growing up with three strong sisters and a mami who ran her own sandwichería in La Paz, Bolivia, little Justa learned early on never to let anyone tell her what to do. Especially not a boy. "Anything you can do, I can do, too!" Justa would say. And she did! Even in basketball, she was a force to be reckoned with. It didn't matter that she was small.

So when she got the idea to be on TV, Justa didn't worry that there was no one else like her anywhere onscreen. She marched up to television stations in her Aymara dress, with her pollera and shawl, looking her very best. And even with one rejection after the next, she didn't give up or try to change. She was determined to succeed.

When she finally got a spot on the news, she became the first Aymara woman on TV. The public loved her immediately! Before long, she created her own cooking show. And, of course, she did things her own way. While mixing together salsitas or her famous fricasé, she would announce, "Mamitas y papitos, I have something to say . . ." She spoke out about racism, violence against women, and defended human rights. She brought many uncomfortable truths to light and inspired national conversations around the dinner table every night.

Her show soon became one of the most popular on TV and she used her fame to help those in need. She cooked for anyone she found who was hungry on the street and set up spaces for women who needed a safe place to sleep. Justa loved cooking, but what she wanted most was to help other women find the confidence to be brave. "La mujer que más les quiere" is still fighting for change today, and she wants her beloved fans to know that she's never going to stop. "There are still barreras que hay que romper!" she says.

EVELYN MIRALLES

VIRTUAL REALITY
ENGINEER

Evelyn Miralles

February 19, 1966—present

It was in little Evelyn's garden in Caracas, Venezuela, where her imagination started to grow wild. Inspired by the TV show *Lost in Space*, she created an imaginary flying saucer with her brothers and sisters that could zoom through the galaxy. Together, they would pretend to land on undiscovered planets and walk around their garden like explorers seeing plants, trees, and animals for the very first time.

When Evelyn grew up, she knew she loved building and started studying to become an architect. But when she took a course in graphic computing, she realized she could build so much more and could create her very own tools, too. She loved thinking of all the new possibilities and began to dream beyond planet Earth. For her final project, she created a 3D model of the NASA spaceship. Her 3D work was so cutting-edge that it caught NASA's attention and they offered her a job.

Soon, she was building NASA's first virtual reality program and the engine it ran on, too. She began creating space environments so that astronauts could prepare for their missions and know what it is like to walk without gravity or any way to tell which way is up or down. Even though Evelyn has never been to space, the experiences she creates are so accurate that, when astronauts go for the first time, they say they feel like they have been there already!

In her office, which is covered in black blankets with glow-in-the-dark stars, Evelyn continues to create new realities every day and is now mentoring other women who want to work in the field. She imagines a future with many more women at her side and hopes they can join her for her next project to get astronauts ready for their mission to Mars!

Selena Quintanilla

April 16, 1971—March 31, 1995

"¡Órale! You've really got it, mija!" said her father as five-year-old Selena sang along with his guitar. Having been part of the music scene for years, Selena's father knew talent when he saw it. He turned the family's garage in Texas into a practice room and taught his children how to play together in a band. "Do we really have to practice?" Selena and her older brother and sister would whine. But when they got on stage at their father's restaurant, they knew it was all worth it. Hearing all the applause and seeing the smiling faces, they were hooked.

There was only one thing left to do: learn to sing in Spanish! "What!? I want to sing like Donna Summer!" said Selena. But when their father insisted, they had an idea. While her brother and sister mixed R & B and techno music into Tejano beats, Selena created her own unique sound, bringing together stylings from Mexico and the United States with a bit of cumbia dancing to shake up the stage.

Soon, Selena y Los Dinos were the coolest band around. They were the life of the party all over Texas and in Mexico, too! Selena felt like she was living a dream. "But it's not only my dream. When I'm up on stage, I feel like I'm singing the hopes and dreams of everyone there!" she said. And she was right. When she became the first Tejano singer to win a Grammy, Mexican Americans all over the United States beamed with pride.

Sadly, Selena died tragically at only twenty-three. Fans from all over the world lined up for a mile to say their goodbyes and vowed to keep her memory and music alive. Selena's spirit lives on whenever a recording of her singing "Ay, ay, ay como me duele" comes on and despite tears in their eyes, people smile and get up to dance.

BERTA CÁCERES
ACTIVIST

Berta Cáceres

March 4, 1973—March 3, 2016

As a little girl, Berta and her brothers and sisters would huddle around their mother's radio and secretly listen to the voices from Cuba and Nicaragua speaking out about equality. Berta's mother knew that these radio stations were outlawed in Honduras, but as the mayor, governor, and midwife in their Lenca community, she needed to keep everyone up to date with pueblos defending their rights.

As Berta grew older, she found her own voice. She studied law and started a radio show like the ones she listened to as a child. She educated her neighbors about their civil rights and created an organization where everyone came together to talk about how best to run their community.

When a big electric company, Sinohydro, came to build a dam on their land without their permission, Berta's pueblo was ready. The company sent in the military, but Berta and her community built a roadblock out of rocks, and day after day, they stood their ground, protecting their drinking water and all the animals who needed the river to survive. After several months, the electric company backed down. Their beautiful, sacred river, "El río Blanco," was safe!

News of their pueblo's victory spread, and when other communities started to resist, too, utility companies tried to stop the movement by sending Berta death threats. But Berta stepped up the fight, traveling to even more communities all over the Americas. "Wake up! There isn't any more time!" she said. "We are the guardians of the land and rivers, and it is up to us to protect them for future generations." Sadly, Berta was assassinated. But by then, her ideas had already spread far and wide. Pueblos everywhere were ready to take on la lucha, determined to honor Berta's memory.

Serena Auñón

April 9, 1976—present

From the time Serena first watched a space shuttle shoot through the sky, she made up her mind to be one of the astronauts inside. Watching the launch again and again on TV, she dreamed of floating in space and doing somersaults right through the air.

"You know, NASA always needs engineers!" Serena's papi said. And that got ideas buzzing around in her head.

When she grew up, Serena went to college and studied engineering. She loved learning about systems and figuring out how everything connects: how one part works with the next. But hearing her friends in medical school talk about their classes on how the body heals made Serena stop and think: "When we are up in space with no gravity, do things in our bodies change? Are there different rules in outer space, or do we stay the same?"

At the University of Texas, Serena found a program where she could study to become both an astronaut and a doctor. She was so excited to find out what happens to human diseases in space that as soon as she got her degree in aerospace medicine, she applied and was accepted as an astronaut on NASA's team!

On her very first mission in 2018, Serena brought along a sample of cells and proteins, some from patients with cancer and some from patients with Alzheimer's disease. Without gravity, she was able to study the samples in 3D. Her work has only begun, but she is already helping doctors on earth better understand and treat their patients. Now she can't wait for her next missions: she hopes to go to the moon and then, maybe someday, to Mars!

WANDA DÍAZ-MERCED

ASTROPHYSICIST

: Wanda Díaz-Merced :

1982—present

"Five, four, three, two, one . . . blast off!" little Wanda and her sister would yell. And holding tight to their bedposts, they would shoot off into space and spin around Saturn's rings, catch falling comets, and whirl through the winds of Neptune. In their imaginary spaceship, they would sail through the stars, millions of miles from their tiny town in Puerto Rico.

But it wasn't until Wanda won second place in her school's science fair that she started to imagine becoming a real scientist one day. She worked hard so that she could go to college and follow her dream of studying the stars.

Wanda made it to college, but something was terribly wrong. She didn't want to tell anyone at first, but with every day that passed, she was losing her sight. She learned braille and tried to show her professors how to explain to her the graphs and charts that she couldn't see. But as her classmates shot ahead in their studies, she knew she needed to do more in order to succeed. She thought long and hard about it until she came up with an idea. "I could listen to the stars!" she thought to herself. Soon, Wanda went to work turning data points into rhythms, pitches, and tones. Before long, she had created an entire symphony of sounds for the stars, asteroids, and planets!

Using her sonification system, she mapped out the entire electromagnetic spectrum. Then, studying light bursts that even sighted astronomers couldn't see, she started discovering new patterns in star formation that led to breakthroughs in astronomy.

Now, working with a school for people who are blind in South Africa, Wanda is developing her techniques so that every scientist has a chance to shine. As Wanda says, "Science is for everyone and should belong to everyone because we are all natural explorers."

MARTA VIEIRA

SOCCER STAR

Marta Vieira da Silva

February 19, 1986—present

When Marta wasn't selling fruit at the public market to help her family, she was playing futebol at her vovó's house with all her primos. "Why don't you play with dolls? You're a girl!" her vovó would say. But running, jumping, and tumbling through the streets of Dois Riachos, Brazil, with her primos was how Marta loved to play.

Neighbors sitting on their stoops gave her funny looks as she went by. But Marta didn't let any of that keep her from training every day. By ten years old, Marta started playing on a local boys' team. Together, they won the championship two years in a row! Marta was very happy, but one of the other coaches got angry. "If you keep letting that girl play, I'm pulling my team out of the league," he said.

Marta couldn't understand what all the fuss was about. "I'm just as good as any of those boys," she insisted. But Marta was banned all the same. Her coach told her that her only chance to keep playing was to try out for the national women's team in Río de Janeiro. But it would take three days to get there by bus, and Marta didn't want to leave her family . . .

Marta was so scared, but she got on that bus, went to the tryouts, and made the team! She's been playing ever since. She has been the FIFA World Player of the Year six times and holds the record for the most goals scored in the World Cup!

ALEXANDRIA OCASIO-CORTEZ

CONGRESSWOMAN

Alexandria Ocasio-Cortez

October 13, 1989—present

When Alexandria was five years old, her mami and papi decided to leave their family in the Bronx and move to the suburbs. They told her she would have better opportunities at her new school. Alexandria started to see that her zip code could make it easier or harder to be who she wanted to be.

But it wasn't until going on a road trip to Washington, DC, that Alexandria began to dream. As she and her papi sat by the reflecting pool and looked at the Washington Monument and the Capitol Building standing tall against the sky, he said, "You know, this all belongs to us. This is our government, and it belongs to you and me."

Even though many things didn't feel like they belonged to Alexandria—her school where nobody looked like her or all the places she did her homework while her mami cleaned—she believed what her papi said. And when she grew up, she had an idea that could make the government feel like it really did belong to everybody. She decided to run for Congress and took to the streets to register voters and get to know her neighbors' needs. And night after night, she researched and planned. When it was time for her first debate on TV, her opponent said, "You're too young." But she stood up to him. And she won!

At twenty-eight years old, Alexandria became the youngest member of Congress in history. As she fights to make healthcare a right, to protect our environment, and to make public colleges free, she is giving people hope for a country where, as she says, "your zip code no longer determines your destiny."

LAURIE HERNANDEZ

OLYMPIC GYMNAST

Lauren Zoe Hernandez

June 9, 2000—present

In Laurie's house, music framed the days. It marked each new year, when her family and friends would dance right up until the ball dropped at midnight. It marked weekend mornings, when it was time to snuggle up and relax with her papi and his jazz records. And it even marked the cleaning parties, when everyone in her family would drop their mops and brooms to dance.

So, when Laurie started taking gymnastics at five years old, she naturally thought to put her routines to music. Music helped her remember all the different steps and flips. The beats let her know how and when each of her moves came together. But one day, just as she was about to turn on the music for her beam routine, her coach stopped her. "Today, I want you to do your routine in silence," she said. "It's the way it's done in competitions."

Everyone in the gym stopped to watch, and Laurie started to feel shaky. She felt like she couldn't move. But as she felt the beam under her feet, she had an idea. It felt a little strange at first, but she let the sound of her hands and feet hitting the beam mark the beat. She gave each twist, turn, and jump its own rhythm. And before she knew it, she had done her whole routine perfectly!

Laurie went on to do many perfect routines following her own beat. She made it all the way from her small gym in New Jersey to the Olympics, where she won silver and gold medals. And, since she had always loved to dance, she tried out for *Dancing with the Stars* and won that competition, too! Now, as she thinks of all of the wonderful possibilities for what she will do next, she feels strong knowing that she has everything she needs inside of herself. Whether she decides to compete a second time in the Olympics, goes on to become a dancer or an actress, or discovers a new path she hasn't even dreamed up yet, she knows, as she decided that day for her first silent routine, "I got this!"

⋆ More Latinitas ⋆

There are so many stories of inspiring Latinas across the United States
and throughout Latin America, and I wish I could write about them all!
Here are just a few of the other Latinitas that I wanted to share with you.
I hope they encourage you to discover even more on your own!

★ ★

Leona Vicario
1789–1842
Leader in the war for independence and
informant for the rebels. One of the first
female journalists in Mexico.

Petronila Angélica Gómez
1883–1971
Leader of the first feminist organization
and editor of the first feminist magazine
in the Dominican Republic.

Hermelinda Urvina
1905–2008
First South American woman to become
a pilot and join Amelia Earhart's group
named The Ninety-Nines.

Eva Perón
1919–1952
First lady of Argentina and activist who
advocated for public services and was a
strong supporter of workers' rights.

Mirabal sisters

1924–1960

Rebel activists during President Trujillo's regime in the Dominican Republic and whose assassination sparked a revolution.

Sylvia Mendez

1936–present

First Latina child to desegregate an all-white school in the United States after the 1948 landmark case *Mendez v. Westminster.*

Sara Gómez

1942–1974

First woman film director in Cuba and the first to show revolutionary Cuba through an Afro-Cuban perspective.

Verónica Michelle Bachelet

1951–present

First woman in South America to be democratically elected as president. Elected for two consecutive terms in Chile.

Gloria Estefan

1957–present

Winner of seven Grammy awards for her singing. She also works as a producer supporting Latinx talent.

Ellen Ochoa

1958–present

First Latina astronaut to go into space. Inventor with three different patents for optical systems technology.

: Acknowledgments .

I am so grateful to Macmillan for letting me spend the last year and a half getting to know these incredibly inspiring women and for the chance to bring this collection of stories to life. I am especially thankful to my brilliant and generous editor, Laura Godwin, who has polished away at my words to turn these stories into what she poetically calls "little gems," and my talented designer, Liz Dresner, whose beautiful, thoughtful details fill every page of this book. Many thanks also to Mary Van Akin, Molly Ellis, Rachel Murray, Starr Baer, and the rest of the team at Godwin Books. I feel so honored to have gotten the chance to work with all of you!

None of this would have been possible without my wise agent and friend, Adriana Dominguez, who has poured so much love into this book from the very beginning, hopping on the phone day and night to talk about everything from Latinx identity politics to font colors to how I am doing.

Muchísimas, muchísimas gracias to Luis de León Díaz, who has been there for everything— from brainstorming ideas with me to helping me edit my Photoshop files to bringing me tecitos late into the night.

To my Irish American mother, who traveled back to the United States while pregnant with me so that I could one day be president, but could not be happier about me publishing this book. To my two older sisters, Lisa and Jessica Menéndez, who were my first role models and who I am still trying to live up to. To my Guatemalan father and his family of artists, who never told me my art was any good until it was. And to my friends whose excitement about this project has kept me going. Thank you!

An enormous thank-you to everyone who delved into this research long before I did. I particularly want to thank all of the Latinas who carefully guarded records, letters, photos, and documents, wrote their thesis dissertations on these women, and created beautiful documentaries to honor their spirits before they left us. A special thank-you to Balbina Herrera and Dania Batista, who generously took the time to send me treasured pieces of Gumercinda Páez's story, and Emma Otheguy for her amazing insights.

Finally, I want to thank all the women on these pages, whose lives and work inspired me to make this book! I particularly want to thank the architect Susana Torre, who reached out to me in the beginning and whose enthusiasm and support of this project pushed me to make it happen. ¡Mil gracias!

Selected Sources

Sor Juana Inés de la Cruz

Aguilar Salas, Lourdes. "Biografía [de Sor Juana Inés]." Ciudad de Mexico, n.d. http://ucsj.edu.mx/dec/sjm/documentos/biografiaLAS.pdf.

Arróniz, Marcos. 2018. Manual de Biografía Mejicana, ó Galería de Hombres Célebres de Méjico. Alicante : Biblioteca Virtual Miguel de Cervantes, 2018. http://www.cervantesvirtual.com/obra/manual-de-biografia-mejicana-o-galeria-de-hombres-celebres-de-mejico-877891.

Bono, Ferran. "El amor sin tabúes entre sor Juana Inés de la Cruz y la virreina de Mexico." El País, March 30, 2017. https://elpais.com/cultura/2017/03/29/actualidad/1490761165_233141.html.

Colchero, María Teresa. 2006. La Cultura En Movimiento. Puebla, Pue. [Meexico]: BUAP.

de la Cruz, Sor Juana Inés. *Antología poética*. Alianza Editorial, 2007.

——. *El Sueño*. n.d.

——. *Respuesta a Sor Filotea de la Cruz*. n.d. http://bibliotecadigital.tamaulipas.gob.mx/archivos/descargas/31000000339.PDF.

Elorza, Eva M. "Juana Ramírez de Asbaje (1648–1656). El paisaje de la infancia, horizonte inicial." Euskonews, n.d. www.euskonews.com/0602zbk/gaia60201es.html.

Fuller, Amy. "A Mexican Martyr." *History Today*, September 28, 2015. www.historytoday.com/amy-fuller/mexican-martyr.

Grupo Akai. 2019. "Vida De Juana Inés De La Cruz I." NoCierresLosOjos.Com. August 8, 2019. http://www.nocierreslosojos.com/juana-ines-de-la-cruz-biografia/.

Long, Pamela H. "'El caracol': Music in the Works of Sor Juana Ines de la Cruz." PhD diss., Tulane University, 1990. https://digitallibrary.tulane.edu/islandora/object/tulane:27540.

Mexico Desconocido. "Sor Juana Inés de la Cruz: biografía de 1648–1695." *Mexico Desconocido*, November 12, 2019. www.mexicodesconocido.com.mx/sor-juana-ines-de-la-cruz-1648-16951.html.

Morales, Talía. "Vida y obra de Sor Juana Inés de la Cruz." *Aion.mx*, November 12, 2017. http://aion.mx/biografias/vida-y-obra-de-sor-juana-ines-la-cruz.

Vallès, Alejandro Soriano. "La inestimable primera biografía de Sor Juana Inés de la Cruz." n.d. www
.academia.edu/35500178/La_inestimable_primera_biografía_de_Sor_Juana_Inés_de_la_Cruz.

Vázquez, Graciela. "Monografía [Sor Juana]." n.d. http://userpage.fu-berlin.de/vazquez/vazquez/pdf
/monografiaestudiante.pdf.

Juana Azurduy de Padilla

Humboldt Travel. "5 Latin American Women to Celebrate on International Women's Day." *The Humboldt
Current* (blog), March 8, 2018. https://humboldttravel.co.uk/5-amazing-latin-american-women
-celebrate-international-womens-day.

Márquez, Humberto. "Latin America: Women in History—More Than Just Heroines." Interpress Service
News Agency, September 8, 2009. http://www.ipsnews.net/2009/09/latin-america-women-in-history
-more-than-just-heroines.

Museo Histórico Nacional de Argentina. "Juana Azurduy: la revolución con olor a jazmín." Museo Histórico
Nacional de Argentina, Accessed December 1, 2019. https://museohistoriconacional.cultura.gob.ar
/noticia/juana-azurduy-la-revolucion-con-olor-a-jazmin.

O'Donnell, Pacho. 2017. Juana Azurduy. Debolsillo.

Policarpa Salavarrieta

Agaton, Carlos. "Colombia 1817: Las últimas palabras de la heroína 'La Pola' ante de sus verdugos." *Agaton*
(blog), November 14, 2017. https://carlosagaton.blogspot.com/2017/11/colombia-1817-las-ultimas
-palabras-de.html.

Castro Carvajal, Beatriz. "'La Pola', una eterna heroína." *Semana*, November 13, 2018. www.semana.com
/nacio/articulo/historia-sobre-policarpa-salavarrieta-la-pola/540169.

Felipe, Andrés. "Biografía de Policarpa Salavarrieta." Historia-Biografía.com, August 3, 2017. https://historia
-biografia.com/policarpa-salavarrieta/.

Malaver, Carol. "Tras los orígenes de Policarpa luego de 200 años de su ejecución." *El Tiempo*, December
22, 2017. www.eltiempo.com/bogota/libro-que-cuenta-la-historia-de-la-pola-luego-de-200-anos-de
-su-ejecucion-164340.

Molano, Enrique Santos. "Una y mil muertes." *El Tiempo*, November 17, 2017. https://www.eltiempo.com
/opinion/columnistas/enrique-santos-molano/una-y-mil-muertes-bicentenario-de-la-muerte-de-la
-pola-152076.

"Policarpa Salavarrieta." *Biografías y Vidas*. www.biografiasyvidas.com/biografia/s/salavarrieta.html.

"Policarpa Salavarrieta." *La encyclopedia de Banrepcultural*. http://enciclopedia.banrepcultural.org
/index.php?title=Policarpa_Salavarrieta#Biograf.C3.ADa.

"Policarpa Salavarrieta Ríos." *Colombian Culture, Colombia Adoption, and Raising Colombian Kids* (blog),
May 4, 2009. http://raisingcolombiankids.blogspot.com/2009/05/policarpa-salavarrieta-rios.html.

Robledo, Beatriz Helena. *¡Viva La Pola!* Instituto Distrital de las Artes—Idartes, 2009.

Rosa Peña de González

Rodríguez Alcalá de González Oddone, Beatriz. *Rosa Peña.* Academia Paraguaya de la Historia, 1970.

"Una cuestión de familia." ABC Color, August 22, 2004. www.abc.com.py/edicion-impresa/suplementos/abc-revista/una-cuestion-de-familia-780910.html.

Teresa Carreño

Coifman, David. "Bajo la forma de un ángel." Mundoclasico.com, December 22, 2011. www.mundoclasico.com/articulo/16593/%E2%80%9CBajo-la-forma-de-un-%C3%A1ngel%E2%80%9D.

Goedder, Carlos. "Centenario de Teresa Carreño." Centro de Divulgación del Conocimiento Económico para la Libertad de Venezuela. http://cedice.org.ve/centenario-de-teresa-carreno-por-carlos-goedder/.

Gutiérrez, Jesús Eloy. *La página de Teresa* (blog). https://lapaginadeteresa.blogspot.com/.

"Idealism in Music Study: An Interview Secured Expressly for *The Etude* with Noted Piano Virtuoso Mme. Teresa Carreño." *The Etude*, June 1917. https://digitalcommons.gardner-webb.edu/cgi/viewcontent.cgi?article=1635&context=etude.

Kijas, Anna. *Documenting Teresa Carreño* (blog). https://documentingcarreno.org/resources.

Milinowski, Marta. *Teresa Carreño, "by the Grace of God."* Forgotten Books, 2018.

Murley, Katherine. "History Hunt: Teresa Carreño." *Katherine Murley's Music Studio Blog* (blog), August 28, 2015. https://kamurley.wordpress.com/2015/08/28/history-hunt-teresa-carreno/.

Rojo, Violeta. "Teresa Carreño. Una Biografía Autoreferencial." Universidad Simón Bolívar División de Ciencias Sociales y Humanidades, Departamento de Lengua y Literatura, September 2006. https://studylib.es/doc/5873949/teresa-carre%C3%B1o-una-biograf%C3%ADa-autorreferencial.

"Teresa Carreño Plays Chopin Ballade No. 1 in G Minor Op. 23." Posted by gullivior, October 8, 2010. YouTube video, 8:18. https://www.youtube.com/watch?v=_SCoheEblpo.

Wilson, G. Mark. "Teresa Carreño—Observations in Piano Playing." *The Etude*, February 1914. https://etudemagazine.com/etude/1914/02/teresa-carreno---observations-in-piano-playing.html.

Zelia Nuttall

Adams, Amanda. *Ladies of the Field: Early Women Archaeologists and Their Search for Adventure.* Vancouver: Greystone Books, 2010.

Diderich, Peter. "Assessing Ross Parmenter's Unpublished Biography about Zelia Nuttall and the Recovery of Mexico's Past." Newsletter of the History of Archaeology Interest Group, Society for American Archaeology 3, no. 3 and 4 (January 2013). https://www.saa.org/Portals/0/SAA/ABOUTSAA/interestgroups/haig/SAA%20HAIG%20newsletter_v3_no3.pdf.

Nuttall, Zelia. "The Terracotta Heads of Teotihuacan." *The American Journal of Archaeology and of the History of the Fine Arts* 2 (April 1, 1886). https://archive.org/stream/jstor-495843/495843#page/n1/mode/2up.

Tozzer, Alfred M. "Zelia Nuttall Obituary." *American Anthropologist* (July–September 1933). http://www
.americanethnography.com/article.php?id=40.

Valiant, Seonaid. *Ornamental Nationalism: Archaeology and Antiquities in Mexico, 1876–1911*. Brill, n.d.

Yount, Lisa. *A to Z of Women in Science and Math*. New York: Facts on File, 2007.

Antonia Navarro

Cañas Dinarte, Carlos. "Ella es la primera mujer universitaria de Centroamérica." *Noticias de El Salvador*,
September 21, 2018. www.elsalvador.com/entretenimiento/cultura/520777/ella-es-la-primera-mujer
-universitaria-de-centroamerica.

———. "La primera abogada de El Salvador." Diario El Mundo, April 1, 2019. https://elmundo.sv/la-primera
-abogada-de-el-salvador.

Hernández, Rosarlin. "Antonia Navarro, la mujer del presente." *Séptimo Sentido*, March 19, 2017. https://7s
.laprensagrafica.com/antonia-navarro-la-mujer-del-presente.

Ligia. "Antonia Navarro, la primera mujer en obtener un título universitario en El Salvador." *Qué Joder*
(blog), December 16, 2018. https://quejoder.wordpress.com/2018/12/16/antonia-navarro-la-primera
-mujer-en-obtener-un-titulo-universitario-en-el-salvador.

Wollants, Mirella. "¿Sabemos realmente qué es educación?" *Elsalvador.com*, December 22, 2018. https://
historico.eldiariodehoy.com/historico-edh/100992/sabemos-realmente-que-es-educacion.html.

Matilde Hidalgo

Benítez Correa, Carmen Delia. "Matilde hidalgo, la mujer que creyó en los derechos de las mujeres."
In *Locas: escritoras y personajes femeninos cuestionando las normas*, pp. 131–44. Arcibel, 2015.
https://idus.us.es/xmlui/bitstream/handle/11441/54699/Pages%20from%20libro%20locas-5.pdf
?sequence=1&isAllowed=y.

Clark, A. Kim. *Gender, State, and Medicine in Highland Ecuador: Modernizing Women, Modernizing the
State, 1895–1950*. University of Pittsburgh Press, 2012.

Estrada Ruíz, Jenny. *Una mujer total: Matilde Hidalgo de Procel*. La Cemento Nacional, 1997.

"Matilde Hidalgo abrió las puertas de una sociedad equitativa en Ecuador." Ministerio de Salud Pública de
Ecuador. www.salud.gob.ec/matilde-hidalgo-abrio-las-puertas-de-una-sociedad-equitativa-en-ecuador/.

"Matilde Hidalgo de Procel." Octubre Noviolento. https://noviolento.wordpress.com/personajes
-de-la-noviolencia/matilde-hidalgo-de-procel-2/.

Gabriela Mistral

"About Gabriela Mistral." Gabriela Mistral Foundation. www.gabrielamistralfoundation.org/web/index
.php?option=com_content&task=view&id=9&Itemid=15.

"Biografía y 15 poemas de Gabriela Mistral." Archivo Chile, Centro de Estudios Miguel Enriquez. www
.archivochile.com/Cultura_Arte_Educacion/gm/d/gmde0004.pdf.

Daydí-Tolson, Santiago. "Gabriela Mistral." Poetry Foundation. www.poetryfoundation.org/poets/gabriela -mistral.

"Documental 'Volveré Olvidada o Amada . . . Tal como Dios Me Hizo' (2014) | Museo Gabriela Mistral." Posted by Gabriela Mistral Vicuña, January 9, 2018. YouTube video, 51:21. https://www.youtube.com /watch?v=OXx6ZsvdhFM.

Figueroa, Lorena. "Tierra, indio, mujer: Pensamiento social de Gabriela Mistral / Lorena Figueroa, Keiko Silva, Patricia Vargas." Biblioteca Virtual Miguel de Cervantes. www.cervantesvirtual.com /obra-visor/tierra-indio-mujer-pensamiento-social-de-gabriela-mistral--0/html/ff1be9f4-82b1-11df -acc7-002185ce6064_40.html#l_1_.

"Gabriela Mistral." EcuRed. www.ecured.cu/Gabriela_Mistral.

García-Gorena, Velma, ed. and trans. *Gabriela Mistral's Letters to Doris Dana*. University of New Mexico Press, 2018.

"Historias de vida—Gabriela Mistral." Posted by Raridades, January 17, 2017. YouTube video, 26:43. https:// www.youtube.com/watch?v=cMAj7taYn4s.

"Lea la última entrevista que Doris Dana concedió a Revista El Sábado en 2002." *Emol*, January 9, 2007. www.emol.com/noticias/magazine/2007/01/09/241650/lea-la-ultima-entrevista-que-doris-dana-concedio -a-revista-el-sabado-en-2002.html.

Mora, Carmen. "Mistral y las vanguardias." Centro Virtual Cervantes. https://cvc.cervantes.es/literatura /escritores/mistral/acerca/acerca_02.htm.

Sepúlveda Vásquez, Carola. "Gabriela Mistral: tácticas de una maestra viajera." *Revista Colombiana de Educación* 61 (February 13, 2011): 281–97. https://doi.org/10.17227/01203916.864.

Juana de Ibarbourou

Fischer, Diego. *Al encuentro de las Tres Marías: Juana de Ibarbourou más allá del mito*. Aguilar, 2008.

Garrido, Lorena. "Storni, Mistral, Ibarbourou: encuentros en la creación de una poética feminista." *Documentos Lingüísticos y Literarios* 28 (2005): 34–39. www.humanidades.uach.cl/documentos_linguisticos /document.php?id=90.

Ibarbourou, Juana de. "Autobiografía lírica parte 2" [audio recording]. Urumelb. http://urumelb.tripod .com/juana/audio-pags/juana-de-ibarbourou-autobiografia-lirica-parte-2.htm.

——. *Chico Carlo*. 1944; reprint, Arca, 2000.

"Juana de Ibarbourou, la poetisa más importante de Iberoamérica." Notimerica.com, July 15, 2017. www.notim erica.com/sociedad/noticia-juana-ibarbourou-poetisa-mas-importante-iberoamerica-20170715081341 .html.

"Juana de Ibarbourou: Menú e poemas sin audio." Urumelb. http://urumelb.tripod.com/juana/menu.htm.

Marting, Diane E., ed. *Spanish American Women Writers: A Bio-Bibliographical Source Book*. Greenwood Press, 1990.

Pickenhayn, Jorge Oscar. *Vida y obra de Juana de Ibarbourou*. Plus Ultra, 1980.

Reyes, Alfonso, and Juana de Ibarbourou. *Grito de auxilio: correspondencia entre Alfonso Reyes y Juana de Ibarbourou*. El Colegio Nacional, 2001.

Romiti Vinelli, Elena. "Juana de Ibarbourou y la autoficción." *Revista de la Biblioteca Nacional* 3, no. 4/5 (2011): 215–29. http://bibliotecadigital.bibna.gub.uy:8080/jspui/bitstream/123456789/31913/1/Juana _de_Ibarbourou_y_la_autoficcion.pdf.

Pura Belpré

Hernández-Delgado, Julio L. "Pura Teresa Belpré, Storyteller and Pioneer Puerto Rican Librarian." *The Library Quarterly: Information, Community, Policy* 62, no. 4 (October 1992): 425–440, www.jstor.org/stable/4308742.

Sánchez Gónzalez, Lisa, ed. *The Stories I Read to the Children: The Life and Writing of Pura Belpré, the Legendary Storyteller, Children's Author, and New York Public Librarian*. New York: Center for Puerto Rican Studies, 2013.

Ulaby, Neda. "How NYC's First Puerto Rican Librarian Brought Spanish to the Shelves." NPR, September 8, 2016. www.npr.org/2016/09/08/492957864/how-nycs-first-puerto-rican-librarian-brought-spanish-to -the-shelves.

Gumercinda Páez

Batista Guevara, Dania Betzy. *Gumersinda Páez: pensamiento y proyección*. Universidad de Panamá, 2011.

Bermúdez Valdés, Julio, and Berta Valencia Mosquera. *Gumersinda Páez*. Protagonistas del siglo XX panameño. Ediciónes Debate, 2015. www.protagonistaspanamasigloxx.com/product/gumersinda-paez/.

Guardia, Mónica. "De maestra a constituyente por elección del pueblo." *La Estrella de Panamá*, January 13, 2019. www.laestrella.com.pa/nacional/190113/pueblo-maestra-eleccion-constituyente.

———. "Neira de Calvo y Gumercinda Páez: mujeres que apoyaron a otras mujeres." *La Estrella De Panamá*, January 6, 2019. http://laestrella.com.pa/panama/nacional/neira-calvo-gumercinda-paez-mujeres -apoyaron-otras-mujeres/24100534.

"Gumercinda Páez." Revolvy. www.revolvy.com/page/Gumercinda-P%C3%A1ez.

Páez, Gumercinda. "[Carta] 1950 ago. 9, Panamá [a] Gabriela Mistral, Jalapa, Vercruz, México [manuscrito]." BND: Archivo del Escritor. www.bibliotecanacionaldigital.gob.cl/bnd/623/w3-article-140553.html.

Frida Kahlo

Donnia. "Rare Pictures of Frida Kahlo's Childhood Taken by Her Father." *Fubiz Media*, 2016. www.fubiz.net /en/2016/02/27/rare-pictures-of-frida-kahlos-childhood-taken-by-her-father.

Herrera, Hayden. *Frida: A Biography of Frida Kahlo*. New York: HarperCollins, 2002.

Julia de Burgos

"Becoming Julia de Burgos: The Making of a Puerto Rican Icon." Posted by Center for Puerto Rican Studies-Centro, July 7, 2016. YouTube video, 1:07:11. https://www.youtube.com/watch?v=_WG46i7P8cY.

Burgos, Julia de. *Song of the Simple Truth.* Curbstone Press, 1997.

Burgos-Lafuente, Lena. "Yo, múltiple: las cartas de Julia de Burgos." Prologue to Julia de Burgos, *Cartas a Consuelo*. Folium, 2014. Via Academia.edu. www.academia.edu/29055390/_Yo_m%C3%BAltiple_Las _cartas_de_Julia_de_Burgos_Introducci%C3%B3n_de_Cartas_a_Consuelo_.

"Cronologia de Julia de Burgos." University of Puerto Rico Humacao. www.uprh.edu/JuliaDeBurgos /cronologia.html.

Echevarría, Norma. *Julia de Burgos: poeta migrante.* Bibliografía Mínima, 2017. www.arecibo.inter.edu /wp-content/uploads/biblioteca/pdf/julia_de_burgos_bibliografia_anotada_2016.pdf.

"Indice de Artículos Digitales: Julia de Burgos." Conuco: Índices de Puerto Rico. www.conucopr.org/Browse. do;jsessionid=542D73F0B6CFDD30BDC8306691B7672D?query=Julia+de+Burgos+%3A+el+vuelo+de +su+ave+fantas%C3%ADa+%2F+Grisselle+Merced+Hern%C3%A1ndez&scope=document_browse.

Martínez, Lizette. "Cartas a Consuelo: ventana al mundo íntimo de Julia de Burgos." Nuestro Rincón de Lectura, January 30, 2019. https://girlybooks.wordpress.com/2019/03/30/cartas-a-consuelo-ventana -al-mundo-intimo-de-julia-de-burgos/.

Mejía, Rosi. "Centenario en honor a Julia de Burgos." *Listin Diario*, September 6, 2013. https://listindiario .com/la-vida/2013/09/06/291101/centenario-en-honor-a-julia-de-burgos.

Olivares, Samuel Nemir. "Entrevista a María Consuelo Sáez Burgos («Cartas a Consuelo: historia inéd-ita de Julia de Burgos»)." *80 Grados*, March 13, 2015. www.80grados.net/entrevista-a-maria-consuelo -saez-burgos-cartas-a-consuelo-historia-inedita-de-julia-de-burgos/.

Puppo, María Lucía, and Alicia Salomone. "'Para entrar a una misma': la espacialización de la subjetividad en la poesía de Julia de Burgos." *Anclajes* 2, no. 3 (2017): 61–76. DOI: 10.19137/anclajes-2017-2135.

Rojas Osorio, Carlos. "Julia de Burgos: la imaginación poética del agua/Un enfoque desde la poética de Bachelard." *Ístmica* 21 (2018): 37–49. https://doi.org/10.15359/istmica.21.3.

Sáez Burgos, María Consuelo. "Julia y Consuelo: binomio de amor," *El Nuevo Día*, January 10, 2015, via PressReader. www.pressreader.com/puerto-rico/el-nuevo-dia1/20150110/282209419233413.

"Sobrina de Julia de Burgos en Festival de la Palabra NY." Posted by Samuel Nemir Olivares Bonilla, June 1, 2015. YouTube video, 6:22. https://www.youtube.com/watch?v=Nw5hFEESEEM.

"Untendered Eyes: Literary Politics of Julia de Burgos." *Centro: Journal of the Center for Puerto Rican Stud-ies* 26, no. 2 (Fall 2014) [special issue]. www.centropr-store.com/centro-journal-vol-xxvi-no-ii-fall-2014/.

"Viva . . . Julia de Burgos." *Primera Hora*, November 13, 2013. www.primerahora.com/videos/vivajuliade burgos-153469/.

Chavela Vargas

"Fallece a los 93 años Chavela Vargas." *El Mundo*, August 6, 2012. www.elmundo.es/elmundo/2012/08/05 /cultura/1344186255.html.

Gund, Catherine, and Daresha Kyi. *Chavela* [documentary film]. Aubin Pictures, 2017.

Mejía, Paula. "Shocking Omissions: The Astonishing Desolation of Chavela Vargas' 'La Llorona.'" NPR, September 4, 2017. www.npr.org/2017/09/04/548113616/shocking-omissions-chavela-vargas-s-la-llorona.

Tuckman, Jo. "Chavela Vargas Obituary." *The Guardian*, August 12, 2012. www.theguardian.com/music/2012/aug/12/chavela-vargas.

Vázquez Martín, Eduardo. "'Les dejo de herencia mi libertad': Entrevista con Chavela Vargas." *Letras Libres*, September 30, 2003. www.letraslibres.com/mexico-espana/les-dejo-herencia-mi-libertad-entrevista-chavela-vargas.

Alicia Alonso

Roca, Octavio. *Cuban Ballet*. Layton, Utah: Gibbs Smith, 2010.

Sanchez Martínez, Martha. "Cumple 97 años Alicia Alonso, la principal bailarina de la región y símbolo de la cultura Cubana." *Nodal*, December 22, 2017. https://www.nodal.am/2017/12/cumple-97-anos-alicia-alonso-la-principal-bailarina-la-region-simbolo-la-cultura-cubana.

teleSUR tv. "Entrevista Especial: Alicia Alonso." December 22, 2016. YouTube video, 25:38. https://www.youtube.com/watch?v=nE2u6XCg_8s&t=2s.

Victoria Santa Cruz

Batalla, Carlos. "Victoria Santa Cruz, la cultura negra hecha mujer." *El Comercio Peru*, October 26, 2012. https://elcomercio.pe/blog/huellasdigitales/2012/10/victoria-santa-cruz-la-cultura.

Bizcel, Dorota. "Victoria Santa Cruz." Hammer Museum, UCLA, n.d. https://hammer.ucla.edu/radical-women/artists/victoria-santa-cruz.

Escobar, Irupé. "Victoria Santa Cruz, la voz de la mujer negra peruana." *La Izquierda Diario*, November 28, 2015. www.laizquierdadiario.mx/Victoria-Santa-Cruz-la-voz-de-la-mujer-negra-peruana.

Ingenio Comunicaciones. "Documental Victoria Santa Cruz-Retratos Parte 1." April 7, 2015. YouTube video, 17:12. https://www.youtube.com/watch?v=Fx4ZiluO6gE.

——. "Documental Victoria Santa Cruz-Retratos Parte 3." April 8, 2014. YouTube video, 11:38. https://www.youtube.com/watch?v=oBRInWFPljo.

Jones, Marcus D., Mónica Carrillo, Victoria Santa Cruz, and Ana Martínez. "Una entrevista con Victoria Santa Cruz." *Callaloo* 34, no. 2 (2011): 518–522. www.jstor.org/stable/41243115.

"La función de la palabra: Victoria Santa Cruz 1." Interview by Marco Aurelio Denegri. Posted by max henry, September 10, 2009. YouTube video, 10:33. https://www.youtube.com/watch?v=TTmiQRsN-fY.

Santa Cruz, Victoria. "Me gritaron negra." Music MGP, April 12, 2016. YouTube video, 3:18. https://www.youtube.com/watch?v=cHr8DTNRZdg.

Santa Cruz Gamarra, Victoria. *Ritmo: el eterno organizador*. Lima, Peru: Ediciones Copé, 2004. https://kilthub.cmu.edu/articles/Ritmo_El_Eterno_Organizador/8321321.

Claribel Alegría

Alegría, Claribel; trans. David Draper Clark. "In Remembrance: The Sword of Poetry (1924–2018)." *World*

Literature Today, January 26, 2018. www.worldliteraturetoday.org/blog/news-and-events/sword-poetry
-claribel-alegria-1924-2018.

Flores y Ascencio, Daniel. "Claribel Alegría." *BOMB Magazine*, January 1, 2000. https://bombmagazine.org
/articles/claribel-alegr%C3%ADa/.

Forché, Carolyn. "Interview with Claribel Alegría." *Index on Censorship* 2 (1984): 11–13. https://journals
.sagepub.com/doi/pdf/10.1080/03064228408533691.

Genzlinger, Neil. "Claribel Alegría, 93, Poet for Central America's Voiceless, Dies." *New York Times*, February
6, 2018. www.nytimes.com/2018/02/06/obituaries/claribel-alegra-central-american-poet-dies.html.

Peralta, Salvador, and Gregory Fraser. "An Interview with Claribel Alegría." *Birmingham Poetry Review* 44
(2017). www.uab.edu/cas/englishpublications/images/documents/BPR/BPR_44/An_Interview_with
_Claribel_Alegria.pdf.

Smith, Harrison. "Claribel Alegria: Central American Poet Who Gave Voice to Struggles in Nicaragua and
El Salvador." *The Independent*, February 8, 2018. www.independent.co.uk/news/obituaries/claribel
-alegria-dead-death-dies-central-america-poet-nicaragua-el-salvador-voice-profile-bio-a8200401
.html.

teleSUR tv. "Fallece en Managua la poeta Claribel Alegría." January 26, 2018. YouTube video, 0:55. https://
www.youtube.com/watch?v=RnXR9WcKjCg.

Watchel, Chuck. "Escape and Tyrannicide: The Extraordinary Stories of Claribel Alegría." *The Nation*, February 5, 2018. www.thenation.com/article/escape-and-tyrannicide/.

Celia Cruz

Riesgo, Vicente, and Hugo Barroso Jr., dir. "Celia Cruz biografía musical." Posted by bauzat, January 23,
2014. YouTube video, 1:31:36. https://www.youtube.com/watch?v=Xila1ozVOKo.

Cruz, Celia, and Ana Cristina Reymundo. *Celia: Mi Vida* (Spanish Edition). New York: Rayo, 2005.

Debocaenboca co. "Celia por siempre." June 4, 2018. YouTube video, 9:17. https://www.youtube.com
/watch?v=uJiYkbU5vh8.

Diaz, GiGi. "Celia Cruz y sus secretos con Omer Pardillo." *Informate con GiGi*, July 28, 2013. YouTube video,
29:00. https://www.youtube.com/watch?v=K7Px21x9Fy4.

Fundación Ernesto McCausland. "Celia Cruz reflexiona sobre la vida." *Una crónica de Ernesto McCausland*,
September 7, 2012. YouTube video, 9:21. https://www.youtube.com/watch?v=EAi-ZxvR6-Y.

RITMO, SABOR Y ESTILO CARACAS. "Confidencias con Celia Cruz 1993." July 30, 2017. YouTube video, 38:00.
https://www.youtube.com/watch?v=zh19UFjWhV4.

Dolores Huerta

Beagle, Christine. "Siete Lenguas: The Rhetorical History of Dolores Huerta and the Rise of Chicana Rhetoric." Dissertation, University of New Mexico, Department of Language and Literature, February 1, 2016.
https://digitalrepository.unm.edu/engl_etds/34.

Bratt, Peter. *Dolores* [documentary film]. 5 Stick Films, 2017.

"Dolores Huerta Grateful for Scout Skills." *Bakersfield Californian*, March 29, 2009. www.bakersfield .com/entertainment/dolores-huerta-grateful-for-scout-skills/article_5d3ff1e5-5615-55eb-b9ee -36dcbf246286.html.

Duarte, Aida. "The Evolution of the Legendary Activist Dolores Huerta: A Look at Her Changing Views on Leadership and Feminism, 1970–2000s." Senior Thesis, Department of History, Barnard College, April 20, 2016. https://history.barnard.edu/sites/default/files/inline-files/AidaDuarte_The Evolution of the Legendary Activist Dolores Huerta_2016.pdf .

Rose, Margaret E. "Dolores Huerta: Passionate Defender of La Causa." California Department of Education—Chavez Curriculum. http://chavez.cde.ca.gov/ModelCurriculum/Teachers/Lessons/Resources /Documents/Dolores_Huerta_Essay.pdf.

Rita Rosita Moreno

Moreno, Rita. Rita Moreno: *Memorias* (Spanish Edition). New York: Celebra, 2013.

——. Interview by Robert Sharp, *Uptown & Country*, Alabama Public Television, January 1981. YouTube video, 15:34. https://www.youtube.com/watch?v=xtrquCPagVs.

Maria Auxiliadora da Silva

Büll, Márcia Regina. "Artistas primitivos, ingênuos (naïfs), populares, contemporâneos, afro-brasileiros: Família Silva: um estudo sobre resistência cultural." Dissertation, Universidade Presbiteriana Mackenzie, August 29, 2007. http://tede.mackenzie.br/jspui/handle/tede/2696.

Oliva, Fernando, and Adriano Pedrosa, eds. *Maria Auxiliadora: Daily Life, Painting and Resistance*. MASP, 2018.

Mercedes Sosa

Christensen, Anette. *Mercedes Sosa: La Voz de la Esperanza*. Tribute2Life Publishers, 2018.

Rohter, Larry. "Mercedes Sosa: A Voice of Hope." *New York Times*, October 9, 1988. www.nytimes .com/1988/10/09/arts/mercedes-sosa-a-voice-of-hope.html.

Isabel Allende

Allende, Isabel. *Paula*. New York: Harper Perennial, 1995.

——. "Enamoured with Shakespeare." In *Shakespeare and Me: 38 Great Writers, Actors, and Directors on What the Bard Means to Them—and Us*, ed. Susannah Carson. London: Oneworld, 2014.

"Isabel Allende." Website. https://www.isabelallende.com.

Susana Torre

Feuerstein, Marcia. "An Interview with Susana Torre." *Reflective Practitioner* 2 (2002). www.susanatorre.net /wp-content/uploads/An-Interview-with-Susana.pdf.

Genevro, Rosalie, and Anne Rieselbach. "A Conversation with Susana Torre." The Architectural League of New York, 2013. https://archleague.org/article/susana-torre/.

Saleri, Nisha. "Feminism by Integrated Spaces in Built Environment." Issuu, February 2, 2018. https://issuu .com/nishatsaleri/docs/feminism_by_integrated_spaces_in_bu.

"Susana Torre." Website. www.susanatorre.net/.

"Susana Torre: Feminism and Architecture." Posted by The Architectural League, January 14, 2015. YouTube video, 48:27. https://www.youtube.com/watch?v=LNNLZgqlghs.

Torre, Susana. Personal communication [email].

Julia Alvarez

Alvarez, Julia. *How the Garcia Girls Lost Their Accents.* 1991; reprint, Algonquin Books, 2010.

——. *Something to Declare.* 1998; reprint, Algonquin Books, 2014.

Karczewska, Anna Maria. "The Mirabal Sisters and Their *Testimonio* in Julia Alvarez's *In the Time of the Butterflies.*" *Crossroads: A Journal of English Studies* 14 (3/2016): 28–36. www.crossroads.uwb.edu.pl /wp-content/uploads/2017/10/crossroads14.pdf.

Stoddard, Fran. "Julia Alvarez." *Profile*, Season 1, Episode 117. PBS, February 18, 2002. www.pbs.org/video /profile-julia-alvarez/.

Sandra Cisneros

Cisneros, Sandra. *A House of My Own.* Knopf, 2015.

Padilla, Gerald. "Interview with Sandra Cisneros." *Latino Book Review*, October 1, 2018. www.latino bookreview.com/interview-with-sandra-cisneros--latino-book-review.html.

"Sandra Cisneros—Early Life." Posted by knopfgroup, March 5, 2009. YouTube video, 3:14. https://www .youtube.com/watch?v=4CuRcFkH9nU.

Sonia Sotomayor

Slen, Peter. "Interview with Justice Sonia Sotomayor." *Book TV.* C-SPAN, January 17, 2018. www.c-span.org /video/?453818-23/book-tv-interview-justice-sonia-sotomayor.

Sotomayor, Sonia. *My Beloved World.* Knopf, 2013.

National Portrait Gallery. "The Four Justices: Justice Sonia Sotomayor Interview—National Portrait Gallery." March 16, 2015. YouTube video, 5:38. https://www.youtube.com/watch?v=PDXrS5nnxsM.

Rigoberta Menchú Tum

Arias, Arturo. "After the Rigoberta Menchú Controversy: Lessons Learned about the Nature of Subalternity and the Specifics of the Indigenous Subject." *MLN* 117, no. 2 (March 2002): 481–505. www.jstor.org/stable/3251663.

Canal Once. "Historias de vida-Rigoberta Menchú." January 15, 2014. YouTube video. https://www.youtube.com /watch?v=xFzk5eLheP8.

Menchú, Rigoberta. *Me llamo Rigoberta Menchú y así me nació la conciencia.* Mexico: Siglo XXI, 1985.

Pontificia Universidad Católica del Ecuador. "Entrevista a Rigoberta Menchú, premio Nobel 1992." November 5, 2018. YouTube video, 12:39. https://www.youtube.com/watch?v=9zXg7c1gAiQ.

RT en Español. "Entrevista con Rigoberta Menchú, premio Nobel de la Paz." October 16, 2014. YouTube video, 28:28. https://www.youtube.com/watch?v=o2dWimUogwA.

Mercedes Doretti

Borrell, Brendan. "Forensic Anthropologist Uses DNA to Solve Real-Life Murder Mysteries in Latin America." *Scientific American*, October 8, 2012. www.scientificamerican.com/article/qa-forensic-anthropologist-mercedes-doretti/.

Doretti, Mercedes. Speech given at the launch of the AAAS Science and Human Rights Coalition. American Association for the Advancement of Science, January 14, 2009. www.aaas.org/programs/science-and-human-rights-coalition/mercedes-doretti.

Economist, The. "Tea with Mercedes Doretti." January 18, 2011. YouTube video, 8:45. https://www.youtube.com/watch?v=jDndRzEF9JY.

Lanchin, Mike. "Digging Up the Truth" [audio recording]. *Witness History*. BBC Sounds, December 5, 2016. www.bbc.co.uk/sounds/play/po4j54ry.

New School, The. "Mercedes Doretti | Commencement Speaker 2016." May 31, 2016. YouTube video, 5:18. https://www.youtube.com/watch?v=2FCNxFi699I.

Shannon, Jen, Chip Cowell, and Esteban Gómez. "How to Care for the Dead" [podcast]. *Sapiens*, November 20, 2018. www.sapiens.org/culture/why-do-we-bury-the-dead/.

Tipett, Krista. "Mercedes Doretti: Laying the Dead to Rest" [podcast]. *On Being*, March 19, 2009. https://onbeing.org/programs/mercedes-doretti-laying-the-dead-to-rest/.

Sonia Solange Pierre

Barnard Center for Research on Women. "Sonia Pierre and the Struggle for Citizenship in the Dominican Republic." December 6, 2012. Video of panel discussion, 1:23:50. http://bcrw.barnard.edu/videos/sonia-pierre-and-the-struggle-for-citizenship-in-the-dominican-republic/.

Bénodin, Robert. "Participé en los movimientos estudiantiles en Villa Altagracia." *Diario Libre*, April 23, 2017. www.diariolibre.com/actualidad/participe-en-los-movimientos-estudiantiles-en-villa-altagracia-EKDL133043.

Chery, Dady. "Interviews of Sonia Pierre, in Memoriam | Entrevistas de Sonia Pierre, in Memoriam." *Haiti Chery* (blog), December 8, 2011. www.dadychery.org/2011/12/08/interviews-of-sonia-pierre-in-memoriam/.

Corcino, Panky. "Sonia Pierre: \'¡Estoy convencida de que lo que estoy haciendo no está mal!\'." *América Latina En Movimiento*, April 16, 2017. www.alainet.org/es/active/16981.

"Expresan su solidaridad con Sonia Pierre." *Diario Digital RD*, April 22, 2007. https://diariodigital.com.do/2007/04/11/expresan-su-solidaridad-con-sonia-pierre.html.

Gamboa, Liliana, and Indira Goris. "Remembering Sonia Pierre, Human Rights Defender." Open Society Foundations: Voices, December 5, 2011. www.opensocietyfoundations.org/voices/remembering-sonia-pierre-human-rights-defender.

Jackson, Regine O. *Geographies of the Haitian Diaspora*. Routledge, 2011, pp. 69–70.

Kane, Gregory. "Sonia Pierre Has a Story for You." *AfricanAmerica.org* (blog), January 4, 2007. www.africanamerica.org/topic/sonia-pierre-has-a-story-for-you.

Katz, Jonathan M. "What Happened When a Nation Erased Birthright Citizenship." *The Atlantic*, November 12, 2018. www.theatlantic.com/ideas/archive/2018/11/dominican-republic-erased-birthright-citizenship/575527/.

"La líder: Sonia Pierre." MUDHA. http://mudhaong.org/quienes-somos/la-lider-sonia-pierre/.

"MRG Expresses Condolences over the Death of Human Rights Activist Sonia Pierre" [press release]. Minority Rights Group, December 13, 2011. https://minorityrights.org/2011/12/13/mrg-expresses-condolences-over-the-death-of-human-rights-activist-sonia-pierre/.

Pierre, Sonia. "Depuración étnica en el Caribe." *El Nuevo Diario*, May 23, 2009. www.elnuevodiario.com.ni/opinion/48369-depuracion-etnica-caribe/.

Rojas, Lissette. "Sonia Pierre, una valiente que enfrentó las miserias materiales y espirituales." *Acento*, December 5, 2011. https://acento.com.do/2011/actualidad/9895-sonia-pierre-una-valiente-que-enfrento-las-miserias-materiales-y-espirituales/.

Rosario Adames, Fausto. "Sonia Pierre: 'El lazo que tengo con esta tierra es lo importante.'" *Acento*, December 4, 2011. https://acento.com.do/2011/actualidad/9847-sonia-pierre-el-lazo-que-tengo-con-esta-tierra-es-lo-importante/.

Santos, Emmanuel. "Sonia Pierre's Struggle for Justice." *Socialist Worker*, January 1, 2007. http://socialistworker.org/2007-1/634/634_04_SoniaPierre.php.

Semple, Kirk. "Dominican Court's Ruling on Citizenship Stirs Emotions in New York." *New York Times*, October 18, 2013. www.nytimes.com/2013/10/18/nyregion/dominican-courts-ruling-on-citizenship-stirs-emotions-in-new-york.html.

"Sonia Pierre." *Periodismohumano*. https://periodismohumano.com/mujer/sonia-pierre.html.

"Sonia Pierre and Dominicans of Haitian Descent: 'We Are Being Erased as Human Beings.'" Latin America Working Group. www.lawg.org/sonia-pierre-and-dominicans-of-haitian-descent-we-are-being-erased-as-human-beings/.

"Sonia Pierre: 2006, Dominican Republic." Robert F. Kennedy Human Rights. https://rfkhumanrights.org/people/sonia-pierre.

"Sonia Pierre: entrevista." Posted by Casa de América, May 13, 2010. YouTube video, 5:31. https://www.youtube.com/watch?v=Hm-LFKR3HLY.

"Sonia Pierre to Receive International Women of Courage Award." *Repeating Islands*, March 6, 2010. https://repeatingislands.com/2010/03/06/sonia-pierre-to-receive-international-women-of-courage-award/.

Justa Canaviri

Aguirre, Liliana. "Justa Canaviri: 'El golpe en la cara se borra, pero el que te llega al alma no.'" *La Razón*, January 7, 2014. www.la-razon.com/tv-radio/Entrevista-Justa_Canaviri-golpe-borra-llega -alma_0_2157384356.html.

Avedaño, Alberto. "La valentía boliviana de 'La Justa' estuvo en DC." *El Tiempo Latino*, January 19, 2015. http://eltiempolatino.com/news/2015/aug/19/la-valentia-boliviana-de-la-justa-estuvo-en-dc/.

Colanzi, Liliana. "La rebelión de las cholas." *El País Semanal*, April 16, 2015. http://elpais.com/elpais /2015/04/10/eps/1428661748_198900.html.

de los Reyes, Ignacio. "La chef que revoluciona la televisión boliviana." BBC News Mundo, October 28, 2014. www.bbc.com/mundo/video_fotos/2014/10/141023_bolivia_chola_presentadora_television_amv.

García Recoaro, Nicolás. "Las cholas y su mundo de polleras." Cuadernos del Centro de Estudios en Diseño y Comunicación 47 (2014): 181–86. https://dialnet.unirioja.es/servlet/articulo?codigo=5232263.

"Justa Canaviri Choque." Television, Radio y Periodicos (blog), October 31, 2010. http://televisionenbolivia .blogspot.com/2010/10/justa-canaviri-choque.html.

"La elegida." La Maja Barata (blog), April 18, 2011. https://lamajabarata.blogspot.com/2011/04/memorias -del-pie-izquierdola-elegida.html.

"La Justa preparación de sajta paceña." Posted by victor marcelo gonzales, July 6, 2015. YouTube video, 5:55. https://www.youtube.com/watch?v=81_rfgVD_IM.

Soruco, Jorge. "Bochornos escolares inolvidables." La Razón, January 9, 2102. www.la-razon.com/suple mentos/mia/Bochornos-escolares-inolvidables_0_1543645715.html.

Evelyn Miralles

Andrea González. "Andrea González presenta la historia de Evelyn Miralles para latinas de éxito en Univi-sion34." July 28, 2018. YouTube video, 3:08. https://www.youtube.com/watch?v=2suhLy2vkM8.

Carson, Erin. "NASA Shows the World Its 20-Year Virtual Reality Experiment to Train Astronauts: The In-side Story." *TechRepublic*, September 17, 2015. https://www.techrepublic.com/article/nasa-shows-the -world-its-20-year-vr-experiment-to-train-astronauts.

CNET en Español. "Evelyn Miralles: Usando la realidad virtual para llevar astronautas al espacio." Septem-ber 20, 2016. YouTube video, 3:17. https://www.youtube.com/watch?v=q5VjEluDeuo.

How to Create VR. "Podcast | E50 | How NASA Uses VR and AR for Training | Evelyn Miralles." February 5, 2019. YouTube video, 32:04. https://www.youtube.com/watch?v=wTFo8j6ngA8.

ideaXme. "Evelyn Miralles, Visionary Innovator at NASA." April 15, 2018. YouTube video, 23:25. https://www .youtube.com/watch?v=fPXpBOQNUi8.

Selena Quintanilla

Early Show, The. "Interview with Selena's Family in 2002." CBS. Posted by Selena World, August 5, 2015. YouTube video, 5:04. https://www.youtube.com/watch?v=a-HlQN78Mdo.

Entertainment Tonight. "EXCLUSIVE: 'Selena' Turns 20! Her Family Reflects on Movie & Legacy: 'In My Mind She's Still Alive.'" March 21, 2017. YouTube video, 9:25. https://www.youtube.com/watch?v=VbR9iFwoXRA.

Latin Trends. "What You Didn't Know About Selena." May 1, 2020. https://latintrends.com/what-you-didnt-know-about-selena.

Mister Golightly. "Selena from 4 Years Old to 23 Years Old (1975–1995)." March 31, 2018. YouTube video, 24:05. https://www.youtube.com/watch?v=1-LFDzBvZhY.

National Museum of American History. "Selena Interview, 1994." September 14, 2017. YouTube video, 2:35. https://www.youtube.com/watch?v=cVN5akAeLo8.

Perez, Chris. *To Selena, with Love*. New York: Celebra, 2012.

"Selena en *Cristina* (part 1)." Posted by selenaripforeverpage. August 25, 2009. YouTube video, 9:09. https://www.youtube.com/watch?v=3Bi1GZMp3uk.

"Selena Interview When She Was a Kid." Posted by ereyes312. August 22, 2010. YouTube video, 1:27. https://www.youtube.com/watch?v=bDcsRcu8YpY.

Sutherland, William. "Selena Quintanilla Perez Biography." Selena Forever website. Accessed December 2, 2019. http://www.selenaforever.com/Selenamusic/selena_biography.html.

Berta Cáceres

Bell, Beverly. "¡Berta Lives! The Life and Legacy of Berta Cáceres." *Food First*, March 9, 2016. https://foodfirst.org/berta-lives-the-life-and-legacy-of-berta-caceres/.

"Berta Cáceres: Con Sus Propias Palabras." Posted by Skylight, September 22, 2016. YouTube video, 3:17. https://www.youtube.com/watch?v=dVKBYbZXCvg.

"Berta Cáceres, la indígena defensora de la naturaleza en Honduras." *Semana Sostenible*, September 16, 2015. https://sostenibilidad.semana.com/impacto/articulo/berta-caceres-desarrollo-como-sinonimo-vida/33854.

Fireside, Daniel. "In the Trenches with Berta Cáceres" *Medium*, April 25, 2016. https://medium.com/@dfireside/in-the-trenches-with-berta-caceres-587da232379e.

Goldman Environmental Prize. "Berta Cáceres Acceptance Speech, 2015 Goldman Prize Ceremony." April 22, 2015. YouTube video, 3:19. https://www.youtube.com/watch?v=AR1kwx8boms.

Hammer Museum. "Berta Vive: Berta Cáceres and the Fight for Indigenous Water Rights." October 29, 2018. YouTube video, 1:49:18. https://www.youtube.com/watch?v=W7kbg3W_n9Y.

Navarro, Santiago; Heriberto Paredes; and Aldo Santiago. "Berta Cáceres, una vida de lucha integral en Honduras." *SubVersiones*, March 4, 2016. https://subversiones.org/archivos/121776.

Pearce, Fred. "In Honduras, Defending Nature Is a Deadly Business." *Yale Environment 360*, February 28, 2017. https://e360.yale.edu/features/honduras-berta-caceres-murder-activists-environmentalists-at-risk.

Romero, Victoria. "Una historia valiente: Berta Cáceres." Amnistia Internacional Venezuela, February 28, 2018. www.amnistia.org/ve/blog/2018/02/5075/una-historia-valiente-berta-caceres.

Villacorta, Orus. "Las mil vidas de Berta Cáceres." *Revista Factum*, June 3, 2016. http://revistafactum.com/berta-caceres/.

Serena Auñón

"Astronaut Friday: Serena Aunon-Chancellor." *Space Center Houston* (blog), August 10, 2018. https://spacecenter.org/astronaut-friday-serena-aunon-chancellor/.

Attanasio, Cedar. "NASA Latina Astronauts: Meet Serena M. Auñón and Ellen Ochoa, 'Reinas de STEM.'" *Latin Times*, March 6, 2915. www.latintimes.com/nasa-latina-astronauts-meet-serena-m-aunon-and-ellen-ochoa-reinas-de-stem-301203.

GW SEAS. "How Do I Become an Astronaut?" February 12, 2013. YouTube video, 57:14. https://www.youtube.com/watch?v=ELwPSTBlCQM.

Puga, Kristina. "Innovator: Serena Auñón, Physician and Astronaut." NBC Latino, September 19, 2013. http://nbclatino.com/2013/09/19/innovator-serena-aunon-physician-and-astronaut/.

Thompson, Andrea. "Medicine in Space: What Microgravity Can Tell Us about Human Health." *Scientific American*, August 7, 2019. www.scientificamerican.com/article/medicine-in-space-what-microgravity-can-tell-us-about-human-health/.

Wanda Díaz-Merced

Díaz-Merced, Wanda. "The Sounds of Science." Institute of Physics, June 2011. www.iop.org/careers/workinglife/articles/page_51170.html.

——. "Making Astronomy Accessible for the Visually Impaired." *Scientific American*, September 22, 2014. https://blogs.scientificamerican.com/voices/making-astronomy-accessible-for-the-visually-impaired/.

Hendrix, Susan. "Summer Intern from Puerto Rico Has Sunny Perspective." NASA, April 28, 2011. www.nasa.gov/centers/goddard/about/people/Wanda_Diaz-Merced.html.

"How Can We Hear the Stars?" *TED Radio Hour*. NPR, January 19, 2017. www.npr.org/2017/01/20/510612425/how-can-we-hear-the-stars.

Koren, Marina. "How Blind Astronomers Will Observe the Solar Eclipse." *The Atlantic*, August 5, 2017. www.theatlantic.com/science/archive/2017/08/experiencing-eclipses-without-seeing/535551/.

Simón, Yara. "This Blind Boricua Astrophysicist Pioneered a Revolutionary Way to Study Stars Through Sound." *Remezcla*, August 25, 2016. https://remezcla.com/features/culture/puerto-rican-astrophysicist-stars-sound/.

TED. "How a Blind Astronomer Found a Way to Hear the Stars | Wanda Diaz Merced." July 13, 2016. YouTube video, 11:15. https://www.youtube.com/watch?v=-hY9QSdaReY.

"This Blind Astrophysicist 'Sees' the Universe in the Most Amazing Way." *National Geographic*/Emic Films, September 21, 2017. www.nationalgeographic.com/video/shorts/1049215555588/.

"Wanda Díaz, la astrofísica ciega que descubre los secretos del universo escuchando las estrellas." BBC Mundo Ciencia, June 21, 2017. www.bbc.com/mundo/noticias-40357876.

Marta Vieira da Silva

Cavalheiro, Gabriela. "Marta—The Interview," *FutebolCidade* (blog), May 5, 2015. http://futebolcidade .com/marta-the-interview/.

Jardim, Claudia. "A Woman's Game: Marta Vieira da Silva" [video]. Al Jazeera, June 24, 2018. www.aljazeera .com/indepth/features/woman-game-marta-vieira-da-silva-180624110229451.html.

"Marta—Orlando Pride and Brazil—BBC Interview for Women's Award." Posted by Giles Goford, May 12, 2017. YouTube video, 3:03. https://www.youtube.com/watch?v=mZZDbeG10Io.

Alexandria Ocasio-Cortez

Alter, Charlotte. "'Change Is Closer Than We Think.' Inside Alexandria Ocasio-Cortez's Unlikely Rise." *Time*, March 21, 2019. https://time.com/longform/alexandria-ocasio-cortez-profile/.

Griffith, Keith. "'Girl from the Bronx' Alexandria Ocasio-Cortez, Who Beat High-Ranking Democrat Joe Crowley, Faces Questions over Her 'Working Class' Background after It Is Revealed She Grew Up in a Wealthy Suburb North of New York City." *Daily Mail*, July 2, 2018. www.dailymail.co.uk/news/article -5905247/Girl-Bronx-Alexandria-Ocasio-Cortez-actually-grew-wealthy-Westchester-County.html.

Lears, Rachel. *Knock Down the House* [documentary film]. Jubilee Films, 2019.

Ma, Alexander, and Eliza Relman. "Meet Alexandria Ocasio-Cortez, the Millennial, Socialist Political Novice Who's Now the Youngest Woman Ever Elected to Congress." *Business Insider*, January 8, 2019. www .businessinsider.com/all-about-alexandria-ocasio-cortez-who-beat-crowley-in-ny-dem- primary-2018-6.

Relman, Eliza. "The Truth about Alexandria Ocasio-Cortez: The Inside Story of How, in Just One Year, Sandy the Bartender Became a Lawmaker Who Triggers Both Parties." *Insider*, January 6, 2019. www.insider .com/alexandria-ocasio-cortez-biography-2019-1.

Shaw, Michael. "The Visual Power of Alexandria Ocasio-Cortez." *Columbia Journalism Review*, April 22, 2019. www.cjr.org/analysis/alexandria-ocasio-cortez-aoc.php.

Wang, Vivian. "Alexandria Ocasio-Cortez: A 28-Year-Old Democratic Giant Slayer." *New York Times*, June 27, 2018. www.nytimes.com/2018/06/27/nyregion/alexandria-ocasio-cortez.html.

Laurie Hernandez

Bruner, Raisa. "Laurie Hernandez and Her Dancing with the Stars Partner Have the Sickest Secret Handshake." *Time*, September 1, 2016. https://time.com/4476393/laurie-hernandez-dancing-with-the -stars-video/.

BUILD Series. "Laurie Hernandez Drops By to Talk About JCPenney's Obsess Clothing Line." April 12, 2018. YouTube video, 25:13. https://www.youtube.com/watch?v=sn_nSnY1L44.

BUILD Series. "Laurie Hernandez Talks Her Children's Book, 'She's Got This.'" October 11, 2018. YouTube video, 16:40. https://www.youtube.com/watch?v=REYGLFlBPfc.

Echegaray, Luis Miguel. "Laurie Hernandez: The US Latina Gymnast with Dreams of Olympic Glory." *The*

Guardian, July 8, 2016. https://www.theguardian.com/sport/2016/jul/08/laurie-hernandez-usa-olympic
-gymnastics-trials.

Gomez, Patrick. "Laurie Hernandez Admits She Missed Out on Childhood for Gymnastics—but Doesn't Re-
gret Her Choice." *People*, January 19, 2017. https://people.com/celebrity/laurie-hernandez-childhood
-gymnastics-no-regrets/.

Hernandez, Laurie. *I Got This: To Gold and Beyond*. New York: HarperCollins, 2017.

——. *She's Got This*. Illustrated by Nina Mata. New York: HarperCollins, 2018.

Insider, The. "Family Confidential: Laurie Hernandez and Her Parents Definitely 'Got This.'" January 25, 2017.
YouTube video, 2:07. https://www.youtube.com/watch?v=WtPwFpSLsT4.

Larson, Greg. "For the Hernandez Family, Raising a Balanced Daughter Was Primary––Laurie's Olympic
Career Is Just a Bonus." US Glove, November 21, 2019. https://www.usglove.com/blogs/news/laurie
-hernandez-family.

Self. "Olympic Gymnast Laurie Hernandez on How Her Mother's Support Helped Her Win Gold." May 11,
2017. YouTube video, 2:03. https://www.youtube.com/watch?v=jdjmsOBKnFE.]

General References on Latinx Identity

Comas-Díaz, Lillian. "Hispanics, Latinos, or Americanos: The Evolution of Identity." *Cultural Diversity and
Ethnic Minority Psychology* 7, no. 2 (2001): 115–120. https://doi.org/10.1037/1099-9809.7.2.115.

Vega, Karrieann Soto, and Chávez, Karma R. "Latinx Rhetoric and Intersectionality in Racial Rhetorical
Criticism." *Communication and Critical/Cultural Studies* 15, no. 4 (2018): 319–325. https://doi.org/10.1
080/14791420.2018.1533642.

Quote Sources

Policarpa Salavarrieta

"I may be a woman": Molano, *Una y mil muertes*

Teresa Carreño

"¡No! Soy Teresita the First!": Milinowski, *Teresa Carreño*

Gabriela Mistral

"This award belongs to my homeland": Gabriela Mistral's Nobel Prize acceptance speech

Juana de Ibarbourou

"Let's go to the campo.": Juana de Ibarbourou, "Vida Aldeana," from *Las Lenguas de Diamante*

Julia de Burgos

"I'm curling the campo's hair!": Olivares, "Entrevista a María Consuelo Sáez Burgos"

Chavela Vargas

"I leave with Mexico in my heart.": *El Mundo*, "Fallece a los 93 años"

Victoria Santa Cruz

"If that negra is going to play": *Documental Victoria Santa Cruz-Retratos Parte 1*

"Porque, in the end": *Documental Victoria Santa Cruz-Retratos Parte 1*

Claribel Alegría

"This isn't right!": Peralta and Fraser, *Birmingham Poetry Review*

"You have the gift of words.": Alegría, "In Remembrance"

"Every time I name them": "Every Time" by Claribel Alegría, translated by Carolyn Forché

Dolores Huerta

"¡Sí se puede!": phrase trademarked by the UFW, https://doloreshuerta.org/faqs/

Maria Auxiliadora da Silva

"I am an artist": Olivia and Pedrosa, *Maria Auxiliadora*

Julia Alvarez

"A bullfighter!": Alvarez, *Something to Declare*

Justa Canaviri

"Mamitas y papitos": Justa Canaviri, opening to her television show

Selena Quintanilla

"Ay, ay, ay como me duele": Selena, "Como la Flor"

Berta Cáceres

"Wake up! There isn't any more time!": Cáceres, Goldman Prize acceptance speech

"We are the guardians": This quote is paraphrased from Berta Cáceres's Goldman Prize acceptance speech

Serena Auñon

"You know, NASA always needs engineers!": GW SEAS, "How Do I Become an Astronaut?"

Wanda Díaz-Merced

"Science is for everyone": TED, "How a Blind Astronomer"

Alexandria Ocasio-Cortez

"You know, this all belongs to us": Lears, *Knock Down the House*

"your zip code no longer determines": Alter, *Time*

Lauren Zoe Hernandez

"I got this!": Hernandez, said at the 2016 summer Olympics and the title of her book

Any dialogue or quote not attributed above is based on the materials found in my sources, but is not historical fact.

HAITI

URUGUAY

BRAZIL

CUBA

NICARAGUA

UNITED STATES

HONDURAS

BOLIVIA